Chindia Alert:

You'll be living in their world, very soon

Zhang Chiahou

Zhang Chiahou

DISCLAIMER

This book: *Chindia Alert: You'll be living in their world, very soon* is for information and entertainment purposes only. Despite our best efforts to provide accurate information, there may be errors. It is also available as a Kindle eBook. And the material is also available without charge from our website *www.chindia-alert.org*.

Before you act on information in this book, you should confirm any facts that are important. We make no warranty as to the reliability, accuracy, timeliness, usefulness or completeness of the information in this book.

We are not responsible for, and cannot guarantee the performance of, goods and services provided by others to whose work we refer. A reference to another author or work does not constitute an endorsement by us.

We have not knowingly infringed any copyright or other intellectual property rights. We attribute our sources where appropriate. If we have inadvertently infringed copyright or IPR, then as soon as the copyright or IPR owner informs us by emailing keeper@chindia-alert.org we will remove the offending material at the earliest opportunity in the next edition.

First published via Kindle – December 2012
First published as a paperback – March 2013

ISBN-13: 978-1482063929
ISBN-10: 1482063921

BACKGROUND AND ACKNOWLEDGEMENT

Although we have been collecting material on China and India for many years, the stimulus to develop the website _www.chindia-alert.og_ and, subsequently, this book was a presentation commissioned by Microsoft in 2006 as the keynote address to their annual EMEA sales and marketing conference in Copenhagen.

We are grateful to Microsoft who has granted us full IPR to the material.

We are indebted to the authors of the articles and books cited in the _Sources_ section at the end; with more significant ones mentioned in the text.

We are also grateful for the content of 100s of websites that we read, many of which are used as hotlinks on our website www.chindia-alert.org and the more significant ones are listed in the _Sources_ section.

ABOUT THE AUTHOR

Zhang Chiahou, China and India watcher, was born in Shanghai and brought up in Calcutta.

Under his Western name, Charles Chang, he has authored numerous management research reports. He is an accomplished speaker and has addressed thousands of business and IT executives across five continents.

He worked for technology firms IBM and Ampex in the US; and for ICL in the UK. Consulting and research followed at Butler Cox, CSC Index, Wentworth Research and Gartner.

He retired in 2005 and started to focus on Chindia watching and research.

He obtained a first degree from IIT, Kharagpur, India and completed his education with Masters Degrees from NYIT and from NYU.

He is a fellow of BCS, the Chartered Institute for IT; and a fellow of the RSA - the Royal Society for the encouragement of Arts, Manufactures and Commerce.

FOREWORD

If you have wondered about where 'China and India' is heading and how it might impact you more than it has already, then this book is for you. It aims to inform and alert you to the threat and opportunities that 'China and India' pose.

This book *Chindia Alert* is derived from a website/blog _www.chindia-alert.org_ compiled since 2006, of the two countries that had the most influence on my formative years. Although I have spent more time in the west since, one doesn't forget where one was born (Shanghai), and where one was brought up and educated (Calcutta).

I am not an economist, an academic or a journalist. I was a management consultant and research analyst for over 30 years (now retired) and I learnt that research is about the ability to locate, read, listen, check, absorb, challenge and synthesize material from a wide range of sources - these are noted on the *Sources* section and also referred to in embedded hotlinks. From these I synthesized what I hope is a coherent picture of the past and present, and a plausible prognosis for the future.

Chindia Alert is not meant to be a static repository of my knowledge and opinions. Rather, I am updating the material – a continuous work-in-progress as it were – through my blog when new inputs arise and new or revised opinions occur to me; or as you offer inputs, corrections or insights - which I intend to include in my blog. Please ensure that any material you send me does not infringe any copyright or other IPRs. I will attribute significant new material, insights or corrections to you. I plan to update this book from time to time when enough changes or new material have accumulated.

THIS BOOK SHOULD BE OF PARTICULAR INTEREST TO

- o <u>Business investors</u> who intend to do business there, and wish to immerse themselves in what motivates and influences local decision making.
- o <u>Politicians</u> and <u>public sector staff</u> who have access to too much information that is not easily digestible, and lack insights into the history and culture of those nations.
- o <u>Media</u> people who are not specialized in China/India who need to develop a relatively quick understanding of the trends in Chindia and how these might affect an area in which they have a specific interest.
- o <u>Professionals</u> such as *lawyers*, *accountants* and *management consultants* who are trying to specialize in the emerging China or India.
- o <u>Business school</u> *professors* and *students* who are not specialists in this area of the world but whose specialisms are increasingly being affected.
- o <u>Holiday makers</u>, particularly those who like to prepare by soaking up as much of the history and culture before spending time there.
- o <u>Joe public</u> whose lives have been impacted by Chindia and whose interest has been aroused by recent developments in China/India.

CONTENTS

1 WHY DO WE NEED A CHINDIA ALERT?

Chindia is a virtual land of China and India. But there are political, ethnic/cultural, economic and geopolitical differences between China and India that, some argue, make the concept of Chindia an inappropriate entity. Hence Chindia will remain virtual - at least for the foreseeable future.

Although Chindia may never become a real entity, China and India individually are having and will continue to have a dramatic impact on the world stage for some time to come. You'll be living in their world – very soon. China and India require serious attention; case of *'hidden dragon and crouching tiger'*. Without this attention, governments, businesses and, indeed, individuals may find themselves at a great disadvantage - sooner rather than later.

There is not only huge interest in China and India, but there is an over abundance of information. You can hardly open a newspaper without at least one article on China or India. However, as we know, having lots of information available does not necessarily make one any wiser.

There are also innumerable misconceptions, myths and even misinformation about China and India.

This book will try to correct these and to make the information more meaningful by putting some order and structure to the information:

o   Starting with a brief recap of the <u>history </u>of both nations - to provide a context for their attitudes towards the West.
o   Examining their <u>social and cultural differences</u> and similarities.

1

- o Moving on to <u>economics</u> post glasnost - uncovering the myth that China is mainly about manufacturing and India about services.
- o Analyzing the <u>political</u> situation - including some serious causes for concern; and a brief geopolitical sit-rep.
- o Giving you our <u>prognosis</u> for the medium-term future.

Why is Chindia a big deal?

'Chindia' is a portmanteau word made up of 'China' and 'India' and refers to them and their economies. The term was popularized in 2005 in *'Making Sense of Chindia'* by Shri <u>Jairam Ramesh</u>, a senior Indian politician in the upper house, Rajya Sabha. However, the term was used in India for a time before.

China and India are neighbors with the Himalayas in between. They are among the fastest growing economies of the world. China ranks 2nd in the GDP for 2011, $7,298bn, and India ranks 10th, $1,827bn. They are destined to change the shape of world economics in the next half century.

The economic strengths of these two countries are considered by many to be complementary: China is stronger in manufacturing and infrastructure, hardware and physical markets; while India is strong in services and information technology, software and in financial and information markets.

{The paragraphs above are derived from <u>Chindia</u> in Wikipedia}

The countries also share certain several historical links - the spread of Buddhism from India to China and trade on the <u>Silk Road</u> are some examples.

Here is a question worthy of *'Who wants to be a millionaire?'*: "What links the three plants: *camellia sinesis, morus alba,* and *papaver sominferum*?"

The answer is: China, India, Britain and the Honorable (sic) <u>East India Company</u> (EIC) with tea, mulberry (silk), and poppy (opium)!

The EIC was founded on December 31, 1600 CE during Queen Elizabeth's reign, the first joint-stock company and had sole (British) rights to trade with India. It became a colonial power in 1757, after the Battle of Plassey - the start of the <u>'divide and conquer'</u> strategy - and lasted till 1857, when as a result of the *<u>'Sepoy Mutiny'</u>* (or first Indian war of independence, 1857), the British government took over.

The British government had not been an idle bystander before then. Col Arthur Wellesley, later to be ennobled as the Duke of Wellington, the nemesis of Napoleon at Waterloo, was instrumental in spreading British rule all the way down to Mysore in South India commanding a British government regiment fighting alongside Company troops. The defeat of Tipu Sultan, ruler of Mysore did much to help spread British rule.

Having managed to dominate trade in India, EIC turned its mind to China. So much of silk, tea and porcelain were being imported into Britain and so little in return was desired by the Chinese that the trade deficit was becoming a major problem. The answer was two-fold: to smuggle tea shrubs to be planted in India and opium, grown in India and sold to the unsuspecting Chinese.

The smuggling of and transplanting tea into India took several years to effect though eventually, British tastes turned to Indian tea in preference to Chinese tea. See excellent book: _For all the Tea in China_ by Sarah Rose.

Concerning opium, the Qing rulers took a dim view of this and the British practiced _'gunboat diplomacy'_ which resulted in two Opium Wars (1839-42 and 1856-60). After which China became a quasi-colony and suffered a _'century of humiliation'_ - see later section on history of China.

This was worse than being a colony as the controlling powers – at one juncture, eight nations, including Japan, attacked Peking - had little desire to develop the country and sought merely short-term gains. Thus was, is, and will be, rampant, unregulated, self-serving, 'winner takes all', capitalism. {Note: we are not referring to Hong Kong which by contrast was run as a colony and hence did not suffer from being treated as Shanghai and other quasi colonies.}

China is the world's most populous country with over 1.3bn people

China has a relatively homogenous population. The vast majority are Han. Politically, China is ruled by a single-party dictatorship (or "people's democratic dictatorship" as defined by Chairman Mao in June 1949).

China is thought to produce 40% of the world's consumer goods; the world's second largest trading nation. In 2009 it overtook Germany as number 1 exporter. For Christmas 2009, an estimated 70lb of toys and games were shipped to UK for every child, heavier than average 9 year old boy. Also, China has a strong lead in international markets and is a major investor in Africa and South America.

Geographically, China is the fourth largest country covering 9.3m sq km and is very fertile along the coastal plains and the three great river systems, flowing west to east:

o   The Yellow River, not far from Beijing
o   The Yangtze, at Shanghai
o   The Pearl River, at Guangzhou.

But there is acute shortage of water elsewhere and only 15% of the land is arable. Inland, there are hostile regions such as deserts like the Gobi in Inner Mongolia and the Taklamakan, and high inhospitable plateaus like Tibet and Qinghai. And mountainous regions like Yunnan and Szechuan.

India is the world's second most populous country with 1.2bn people

India's culture and ethnicity is highly pluralistic. India is a multi-party democracy - the largest democracy in the world. The 2009 Indian national elections drew 700 million voters at 1 million polling stations.

Geographically, India is the world's eighth largest country covering 8.5m sq km. It is very fertile. The population is spread across most of India, including the Deccan plateau and the foothills of the Himalayas. Well over 50% of the land is arable. Only the Thar Desert, in Rajasthan, is sparsely populated.

Being arable is one thing, having enough water is another. Despite great river systems, India's harvest is highly dependent on the annual monsoon. Longer term there is also concern about the shrinking glaciers in the Himalayas, the source of major Indian and Chinese rivers.

Together, a third of the world's population live in Chindia

In economic terms, the commonly-cited complementary nature of China being focused on manufacturing and India being focused on services is becoming outdated as the services sector in China is developing rapidly, while India's manufacturing has grown significantly.

Last but not least, China has greater geopolitical and military clout, as well as a permanent seat on the UN Security Council due to its role in World War II. The other four members of the Security Council: USA,

USSR, Great Britain and France played a direct role in defeating Germany and Japan. China (then *Republic of China*) had little impact, but was included by the US to counterbalance the USSR.

GDP comparison - from <u>Wikipedia</u> and <u>CIA World Factbook</u>

	World	Chindia	China	India
Population m (2011 est US Census Bureau)	7,001	2,548	1,343	1,205
GDP US$ billion (2011, IMF)	69,899	9,125	7,298	1,827
Per capita GDP US$ (2011, IMF)	9,984	3,581	5,434	1,516

2 DIFFERENCES IN HISTORICAL PERSPECTIVE OF THE WEST

Unless one understands the history of a nation, one cannot hope to understand its current affairs and attitudes to other nations. In this chapter we try to summarize pertinent aspects of Chinese and Indian histories.

There is a stark difference in the Chinese and Indian historical perspective of the West. To try and begin to understand that difference:

○ We need firstly to look back, briefly, over the two countries' <u>very long history</u>: China's <u>4,000 years of records</u> and India <u>before the Raj</u>.

○ Then we take a summary look over the turbulent first half of the 20th Century: <u>China transforming</u> from a feudal imperial regime to a republic soon to be wallowing in both a civil war as well as defending against a major foreign invasion; and <u>India transforming</u> from a colonial state to two independent nations immediately to be submerged into post-partition turmoil and conflict which is still there today.

○ And, finally, we look over the 60+ years since: <u>Chinese Liberation</u> – which was almost as traumatic as the first half century; and <u>Indian Independence</u> – relatively placid by comparison, though not when compared to most Western nations.

Before we do that, let's take a quick look at the fundamental differences in perspectives.

Chinese perspective

If you asked a Chinese in Starbucks in Shanghai: *"What is the Chinese view of the West, especially of Britain?"* chances are he will say that, despite never been colonized, China had been mistreated and humiliated by the West, where treaties were one-sided and signed under gunboat diplomacy, that much of Chinese treasures found in western museums and private collections came from the looting of the <u>Old Summer Palace</u> in Beijing 150 years ago towards the end of the Second Opium War (1856-60) waged by Britain - led by the 8th Lord Elgin, son of the Lord Elgin of the Parthenon marbles - and France and that this all resulted from western (British) commercial greed that caused the British East India Company to introduce and sell opium to China to offset the cost of Chinese tea, silk and porcelain.

True Story of Ah Q - is a short novel by Lu Xun, an author of the early part of the 20th century and highly regarded by Chinese of all persuasions - left, right and centre. Westerners should note that this story of Ah Q is remembered as symptomatic of China's past, something that today's Chinese will not allow to happen again. China instituted the <u>Lu Xun Literature Prize</u> in 1995 awarded every three years, along the lines of the British Booker Prize. Incidentally, the Q of Ah Q is named after the pigtail or queue Han Chinese men were ordered to adopt on pain of death by the Manchus (Qing Dynasty).

Ah Q
According to Cultural China>History>Literature – *http://tinyurl.com/bz6j9zc*

"... The 'adventures of Ah Q, a man from the peasant, rural class with little education and no definite work. Ah Q is famous for 'spiritual victories', Lu Xun's euphemism for self-deception even when faced with extreme defeat or humiliation. Ah Q is a bully of the less fortunate but fearful of those who are above him in rank, strength, or power. He persuades himself mentally that he is spiritually 'superior' to his oppressors even as he succumbs to their tyranny and suppression. Lu Xun exposes Ah Q's extreme faults as symptomatic of the Chinese national character of his time."

If western politicians or journalists from time to time say: *"Oh, the Chinese authorities are using this xenophobia to divert local attention away from domestic issue of the day"*, they may only be partly right. There is an underlying and lasting resentment of the century of humiliation which contributed not insignificantly to the descent of China from its position as probably the richest country to one of the poorest in that period, out of which it is now slowly but inexorably recovering. At least in nominal GDP if not yet in GDP per capita.

For a balanced view of the period 1832-1914, you should read: *The Scramble for China: Foreign Devils in the Qing Empire, 1832-1914* by Robert Bickers, history professor, Bristol University.

Indian perspective

If you asked an Indian in McDonald's – *"What is the Indian view of the West, especially of Britain?"* chances are he will say that, despite being subjugated as a British colony, Indians do not hate the British, that the Raj had both good and bad points and, perhaps, with the hindsight of history, the good probably outweighed the bad.

Differences in attitude to historical dating

There is ambiguity of dating in older Indian history as Indian scholars were more interested in the substance and not the chronology of events; and their records, like the Chinese, refers to regnal years. But – unlike the Chinese – there is no cross reference to a continuous calendar such as the Chinese 60-year zodiac cycle.

So until historians of the British Raj started to map Indian dynasties to the western calendar there was some uncertainty as to which dynasty succeeded which other in India. And which rulers of subsets of India coexisted with other such rulers, apart from when wars between them were recorded by historians of both regimes. And it also did not help that there were two great emperors called Chandragupta from two different dynasties - the Maurya and the Gupta - over six centuries apart!

Another example of this lack of interest in 'absolute' time and historical 'fact' also meant that it was British Raj archaeologists like Sir Alexander Cunningham who established the historical Buddha who by the 19th century was regarded more as a legend than a historical person. And the historical temple caves of and at Ajanta, Ellora and Elephanta were discovered by the British; an officer implausibly named John Smith.

Curiously, many British Raj 'scholars' like Sir Alexander were officers in the 'Indian Army'. Good thing there were long periods of stability and peace during the Raj to enable these soldiers to become very competent and enthusiastic archaeologists, historians and surveyors (e.g. Sir George Everest after whom the tallest mountain is named).

Lord Curzon is credited with restoring many of the ancient monuments including the Taj Mahal. His contribution was recalled by Prime Minister Dr Manmohan Singh in his acceptance speech of Honorary Degree from Oxford University, July 8, 2005 London:

In the context of the study and preservation of Indian culture, I also wish to recall the contribution of another great Oxonian, Lord Curzon, about whose project to preserve and restore Indian monuments, Jawaharlal Nehru himself said, "After every other Viceroy has been forgotten, Curzon will be remembered because he restored all that was beautiful in India."

Melding or assimilating

With each invasion of India, the foreign culture was melded into the indigenous one, creating a cultural pluralism. The mixing has not been thorough. For example, the Muslim influence manifests itself even today with Urdu, a derivative Hindustani, with Persian words written in the Arabic script.

It was the Muslim conquerors' systemic effort to communicate with the vanquished. Persian was the Mughal court language, just as Norman French was that of England for several generations after its conquest by Duke William, of Normandy. And the legacy also includes, sadly, periodic Muslim-Hindu rioting, sometimes instigated by unscrupulous politicians such as the infamous destruction by Hindu extremists of the Babri Masjid mosque at Ayodhya built by one of Babar's generals on the destroyed ruins of an ancient temple, and reputed birthplace of Lord Rama.

By contrast, with each invasion of China, the invaders decided that the indigenous culture was so superior that the rulers adopted it, not least because of the established civil administration based on meritocracy. Any peasant could sit the civil service exams, assuming he had enough resources to study and not to till the fields, often through collective financial support from fellow villagers. And over the centuries, several peasants rose to be ministers, though many more became local magistrates and governors.

So the Mongols (Yuan Dynasty founded by Kublai Khan, grandson of Genghis Khan) adopted Han customs and court dress, and protocol - though they appointed mainly Mongols as military chiefs preferred to employ senior civil servants from non-Han peoples, such as Tibetans and Manchus. And several centuries later so did the Manchus (Qing

Dynasty) - again discriminating against the majority Han, certainly for senior military posts but also senior civil servants. This time, inter-marriage between Manchu and Han were prohibited and Han men were required to wear a pigtail (or queue) on pain of death if the queue was shaved off.

2.1   China: four thousand years of records

According to the ancient book Shu Jing, the Book of History, (one of the Five Classics) there has been a 'China' for over 4,000 years.

The Five Classics refer to The Book of Songs (Shī Jīng), The Classic of History (Shū Jīng), The Classic of Rites (Lǐ Jì), The Book of Changes (I Ching), and The Spring and Autumn Annals (Chūn Qiū), all of which are said to be compiled or revised by Confucius.

The Book of Songs is the earliest collection of Chinese poems and it is the source of Chinese verse and the starting point of the Chinese realistic epic. Therefore, The Book of Songs serves as the most valuable and important century B.C.

The Classic of History is a compilation of documentary records related to events in ancient China.

The Classic of Rites is the earliest and most complete record of social hierarchies and ceremonies in ancient China.

The Book of Changes, also referred to as Zhou Yi (Book of Changes of the Zhou Dynasty), is regarded as the most preeminent among all Classics in ancient China.

The Spring and Autumn Annals were the official chronicles of the states during the Pre-Qin Period, however, only that of the State of Lu covering the period from 722 BC to 481 BC survived.

From: Cultural China – Four Books and Five Classics - http://tinyurl.com/d644xao

---

Chinese history begins with the so-called Three Dynasties: the Xia, Shang, and Zhou. Until around 75 years ago, these three dynasties were thought to be legendary. However, since the major excavations at Yinxu (1928-37) where oracle bones naming Shang (1,600 – 1,100 BCE) kings and their diviners, it is now believed to be history as recorded by Sima Qian (145 – 86 BCE) in his Shi ji (Book of the Historian).

The Shu ji also has a list of Xia kings (2,000- 1,600 BCE); including the legendary founder Emperor Yu the Great who taught his people about flood control and irrigation along the Yellow River thereby enabled bountiful harvest to be reaped. Yu is regarded as the grandson of the founding Yellow Emperor. As Xia excavations are uncovering distinct artifacts, the view amongst archaeologists is that it is only a matter of time before the authenticity of the Xia will be confirmed.

For fully authenticated records we start with Emperor QinHsi Huangdi (259 BCE – 210 BCE) - the 'First Emperor' who started to build the Great Wall and whose terracotta soldiers have been uncovered in Sian. He proclaimed that his dynasty would last 10,000 years. But, sadly, it lasted a little beyond his reign. However, the emperor unified China for the first time. Something that would, more or less, last until modern times. He reformed politics, economy and culture. He codified law and established a working tax system. Coinage and measurements were all standardized. The emperor also standardized Chinese writing, which promoted the development of the Chinese culture.

From then, written records of Chinese historical events which - despite major discontinuities due to invasions, rebellions, and revolutions - have been continuous.

Invaders who managed to overcome the indigenous dynasty in power invariably adopted Chinese civil administration, language and culture and within three or so generations became 'Chinese'. Although there were times when several contending regimes ruled over parts of China, more often than not, a single ruler presided over most of what is China today.

China was never colonized per se as India was. But having suffered for over a century great humiliation at the hands of not only many western powers, Britain being the main culprit, but also at the hands of a neighbor, Japan, Chinese have a persistent negative collective memory of foreign powers.

Sixty-year calendar cycle

The historical records usually contain both dynastic and political information such as the reigns of kings and outcomes of battles – which may be hyped by the victor; as well as economic information, such as the yields of harvests and taxation revenues – which are more likely to be factual. The dating of events usually starts from the beginning of a new dynasty – the regnal year.

Fortunately, China has been following a 60-year cycle based on five-element (wood, fire, earth, metal, water) multiplied by 12-zodiac years (rat, ox, tiger, rabbit, dragon, snake, horse, sheep, monkey, rooster, dog, pig). According to tradition, it was invented by *Huang-di* or the *Yellow Emperor,* who is a legendary Chinese sovereign and cultural hero. He is said to be the ancestor of all Chinese. Tradition holds that he reigned from 2697-2597 BCE. He is regarded as the founder of Chinese civilization and pre-dates even the Xia dynasty. The first year of the first 60-year cycle began in 2696 BCE on February 16, by the Gregorian calendar. BTW - this makes the current 2013 - Year of the Snake - year 4,711 in the Chinese calendar.

China has suffered its share of political turmoil over the centuries, sometimes alternating between an indigenous dynasty and one founded by foreign conquerors, such as the Mongols (*Yuan*, 1271 — 1368) replacing Jin (1115 — 1234) or Manchus (*Qing*, 1644 — 1911) replacing *Ming* (1368 — 1644).

Or one dynasty succumbing to over-indulgence and decadence supplanted by another, sometimes triggered by a revolt led by a peasant turned charismatic leader. For instance, the *Tang* dynasty, one of China's 'golden ages' collapsed due a peasant-leader led revolt.

ChinaTown

Incidentally, most big cities have a China Town. The Chinese name for this is Táng rén jiē which means "Tang people's street". Such is the folk memory of the 'golden age' of China that the label sticks even today!

And sometimes, a stable and long-lasting dynasty may splinter into a few contending ones, for a while. But, more often than not, a majority of China would be under a single ruler - see Chinese history timeline. Despite the chaos that prevailed from time to time, there is continuity in Chinese historical records that surpasses that of nearly every other nation apart from, perhaps, Egypt.

Four great inventions of China

China has been the source of many significant inventions including papermaking, the compass, gunpowder, and printing.

Many people are surprised to know that modern agriculture, shipping, astronomical observatories, paper money, umbrellas, wheelbarrows, multi-stage rockets, brandy and whiskey, chess, and much more – including noodles, all came from China. Chinese are materialistic and practical - somewhat different from Indians as we will show on the next section.

This information has been compiled – not by a self-serving Chinese, but - by Joseph Needham, a British scientist and historian, and his colleagues in a study of ancient Chinese books on science, technology and medicine. His research has been published in the yet to be completed, multi-volume, _Science and Civilisation in China_. Some of Needham's work has been condensed in a well-illustrated paperback _The Genius of China: 3,000 Years of Science, Discovery, and Invention_ by Robert Temple.

Needham's original motivation to his research was his doubt that the then purported Chinese inventions could all be Chinese. To his great amazement, his research uncovered more inventions than were previously reported.

2.2   India: Before the Raj

In some ways, Indian (and Pakistani) history goes further back than the Chinese to archaeological sites such as the Indus Valley Civilizations: Mohenjo-Daro in Sind and Harappa, now in Pakistan, dating to 3,000 BCE. In fact only in recent years a new site Mehrgarh has been discovered, deemed to be even older than that of Mohenjo-Daro and Harappa - carbon dating puts it at possibly 7,000 BCE.

But keeping meticulous and accurate records was not deemed to be important. After all, if life is only transitory and according to some Hindu philosophers it may even be an illusion, why bother. [Curiously, recent thinking in cosmology suggests that one possible interpretation of reality is that we are mere 3-D holograms projected from the edge of the universe!] Historical knowledge per se is a kind of unnecessary baggage. Much more important to record the happenings of the past in so far as there are lessons for the present and future.

India has over the centuries, unlike China, experienced a more fragmented past. More often than not, different rajas or sultans ruled over parts of India, even during the height of the British Raj, which at peak ruled over only some 75% of the Indian sub-continent. Again, unlike China, invaders were not absorbed into the local culture and practices. Rather, they often grafted their 'brand' onto the existing - such as Urdu on top of Hindi; and British civil and military processes replacing earlier forms.

Despite the long period of colonial rule, most Indians do not regard the British (or the West) with any animosity. And English is probably spoken by more Indians than Hindi.

Ancient Hindu records

One of India's most ancient records - and some would say the world's - is the _Ramayana_ epic (c 1,000 BCE), part of the Hindu _itihāsa_ ("_it was like this_" or history). In a nutshell, it is about the hero Lord Rama and his wife Sita, fighting and defeating a demon king, Ravana, who was chased to what is probably Sri Lanka. A classical story about good versus evil; when after many trials and tribulations good overcomes evil. However, when one delves into its contents which include monkey troops under Hanuman and so forth, we realize it is more a 'legend' than what one would today regard as 'history'. However, modern archaeologists have traced the itinerary of Rama from northern India to today's Sri Lanka and found evidence that many of the places do exist and some have fragments of Indian Iron Age artifacts.

Similarly the _Mahabharata_ epic (c 800 BCE) is another part of the Hindu _itihāsa_. A basis of Hindu mythology and a major text of Hinduism because, in particular, it contains the hymn _Bhagavad Gita_ (Song of the Blessed Lord), it is immensely important to Indian culture. With about one hundred thousand verses, long prose passages, and about 1.8 million words in total, the Mahabharata is the longest epic poem in the world. It is roughly four times the length of the Iliad and Odyssey combined and about four times the length of the Ramayana. Again, it refers to demons and mythical beings. So, it is not regarded as history by today's standards. Again, modern archaeologists have tried to trace the events which include many battles and, once again, there is geographic evidence that seems to support the story.

First recorded Indian history

Between ancient archaeological ruins (3,000 BCE) and the epics and formal recorded history (300 BCE), historians believe that a central Indo-European race called Aryans (_the noble ones_) migrated into India. These people came from the area between the Black Sea and the Caspian Sea. Some of them stopped in today's Iran, while others continued south-east to today's Pakistan and India. The slow migration did not arrive in northern India until about 1,500 BC.

The written records of the Sanskrit, the language these people brought with them can be read today, and we can see that many words in Sanskrit are basically the same as in other Indo-European languages.

In addition to Sanskrit, the Aryans brought their gods with them to India. These gods form the basis of the <u>Rig Veda</u> and other sagas which were first written down in Sanskrit. They settle down, probably in the Indus Valley, from about 1,500 BC to about 800 BC. It seems to be at this time that the <u>caste system</u> got started. Then they pushed further into India proper. As a result the indigenous people, the Dravidians, were pushed south into the Deccan plateau and beyond.

Although the majority of historians in India and abroad subscribe to the (simplified) pre-history noted above, there is controversy about the Aryan-Dravidian divide, and even some doubt that the Aryans invaded India.

Further Indian records

We have a Grecian record of the battle between <u>Alexander the Great and Porus</u>, King of Punjab with his war elephants in 326 BCE.

But the first history of India as one would regard it today is that of the <u>Maurya Dynasty</u>. This was a geographically extensive and powerful empire in India (321 to 185 BCE) with Chandragupta and <u>Asoka</u> as the most famous rulers. Amongst other achievements of statecraft, Asoka bequeathed his famous non-rust <u>iron pillars</u>, wonders of metallurgy not yet understood today. He also supported Buddhism and some would argue that Buddhism survived because Asoka supported its spread out of India into south east Asia as well as to today's Afghanistan and along the Silk Road as it practically disappeared in India several centuries later. The lions atop his pillars were adopted as the national emblem and the *chakra* is in the middle of the national flag. Incidentally, this dynasty was noted by the Greek traveler <u>Megasthenes</u> in his Indica, which provided the earliest datable accounts.

Even so, it was not until the British looked into the records that they realized that Chandragupta was the name of two very different kings, the first a Mauryan and the second from the <u>Gupta Dynasty</u> (320 – 550 AD) some six-seven centuries later. Like the Tang Dynasty, the Gupta Dynasty is often referred to as a 'golden age'.

Between the Mauryan and the Gupta period, there was a period of 200 years when northern India and Afghanistan, Persia stretching c3,000 miles along the Silk Road were ruled by a central Asian group the <u>Kushans</u>, centered on Peshawar. Their greatest king <u>Kanishka</u> has been recorded in Chinese history.

One of the earliest historical records of India is by Alberuni who wrote about India c1,000 CE. From then on there are records of different empires and dynasties. But only from time to time did a single empire rule the majority of India, such as at height of the Mughal era under Akbar the Great grandson of Babur the Mughal who conquered India. Baber was a descendant of Tamerlane and of Genghis Khan on the maternal side. Abu al-Fazl, the grand vizier of Akbar, was author of the Akbarnama, the official history of Akbar's reign, and also a Persian translation of the Bible.

Most of the historical interest has been centered on northern India. In the meanwhile, south India had a series of kingdoms, such as Cholas, Pandyas, Pallavas, Hoysalas, Cheras, Wodeyars, Chalukyas and the Vijayanagar Empire. The most famous being the Cholas who ruled between the 9th and 13th centuries.

Even at the height of British Raj some 25% of the Indian sub-continent was outside of British rule - see excellent illustrated Indian history timeline by Vikas Kamat. By the bye, it is surprising to many that at the peak, 20,000 British (and many more local) administrators managed the lives of 300 million Indians. Only at Independence did a single authority rule all of India. But by then the North West had been lopped off into West Pakistan and East Bengal had been designated East Pakistan.

Ancient Indian inventions and discoveries

Whereas the Chinese have been credited with many physical inventions, India is credited with many as well including: bangles, buttons, fabrics such as calico (imported by Europeans together with spices' which gave rise to the search for a fast sea route to the 'East Indies' resulting in Columbus 'discovering' the Americas!), chintz and muslin. In addition there were many inventions or discoveries in astronomy and mathematics – pointing to the intellectual nature of Indians.

In **astronomy**, Indians discovered or invented:

o   *Precise celestial calculations*: An Indian mathematician, Aryabhata (c500 CE), accurately calculated celestial constants like the earth's rotation: days per solar orbit, and days per lunar orbit.

o   *Earth goes round the Sun*: Aryabhata was skeptical of the widely-held doctrines about eclipses and also the belief that the Sun goes round the Earth. As early as the sixth century, he talked of the diurnal motion of the Earth and the appearance of the Sun going round.

In **mathematics**, apart from algebra, trigonometry and calculus which originated in India, Indians also developed:

o   *Zero*: Although ancient Babylonians used 'place holders' to distinguish between numbers like 507 and 57, these were no more than blank spaces or sometimes two wedges. The first use of zero as a number and its uses have been found in ancient Indian mathematical treatise.

o   *Value of* π: The value of *'pi'* was first calculated by the Indian mathematician Budhayana, and he also explained the concept of what is known as the Pythagoras Theorem.

o   *Binary number representation*: Another Indian mathematician, Pingala (c100 BCE), developed a system of binary enumeration convertible to decimal numerals. The system he described is quite similar to that of Leibnitz in the 17th century.

o   *'Algorithm'*: Al-Khwarizmi's work, De numero indorum (the Indian Art of Reckoning), was based on an Arabic translation of Brahmagupta. The new notation came to be known as that of al-Khwarizmi, or loosely phonetically translated to *algorismi*. Eventually it came to be called algorithm.

o   Representing large numbers: In his book Cosmos, astronomer/physicist Carl Sagan writes:
    "A millennium before Europeans were willing to divest themselves of the Biblical idea that the world was a few thousand years old, the Mayans were thinking of millions and the Hindus billions."

Indian Classics

Just as the Chinese have their ancient five classics, the Indians (or rather the Hindus) have their ancient classics:
The **Vedas** (Sanskrit: *véda*, "knowledge") are a large body of texts originating in ancient India. Composed in Vedic Sanskrit, the texts constitute the oldest layer of Sanskrit literature and the oldest scriptures of Hinduism. The Vedas are *apauruṣeya* ("not of human agency"). They are supposed to have been directly revealed, and thus are called *śruti* ("what is heard"), distinguishing them from other religious texts, which are called *smṛti* ("what is remembered").
    The Vedic texts or śruti are organized around four canonical collections of metrical material known as *Saṃhitās*, of which the first three are related to the performance of yajna (sacrifice) in historical Vedic religion:
•   The Rigveda, containing hymns to be recited by the priest;

- The <u>Yajurveda</u>, containing formulas to be recited by the adhvaryu or officiating priest;
- The <u>Samaveda</u>, containing formulas to be sung by the priest.
- The fourth is the <u>Atharvaveda</u>, a collection of spells and incantations, apotropaic charms and speculative hymns.

The individual verses contained in these compilations are known as *mantras*. Some selected Vedic mantras are still recited at prayers, religious functions and other auspicious occasions in contemporary Hinduism.

From: <u>The Vedas</u>

2.3 China's Twentieth Century Timeline to mid-century

The first half of the 20th Century was troubled times for China - desperately escaping from imperialism and quasi-colonialism, straight into war with Japan and incipient revolution culminating in liberation.

o 1890s - China is being slowly partitioned by foreign powers. The <u>Boxer Rebellion</u> arises, with stated aim of *"overthrowing Qing and destroying foreigners"*.

o 1899 - Boxers are defeated by Qing, but Dowager <u>Empress Cixi</u> decides they might be useful to her, and sets them task of killing all foreigners in China.

o 1900 - An international force - from <u>eight nations</u> including Britain, USA, Russia, Germany and Japan - arrives in Beijing and routs Boxers. They go on to ransack Summer Palace - a second time.

o 1911 – October 10, <u>Republic of China</u> formed.

o 1912 - Qing dynasty never recovers from humiliations of last 70 years, especially 1900, and eventually collapses. October 10, <u>Sun Yatsen</u> founds Kuomintang (KMT - Nationalist Party) and takes control of new republican government. To avert civil war he offers presidency to Yuan Shikai, former head of Qing armies, and warlord of Northern China.

o 1913 - Yuan dissolves republican government and sends Sun into exile again.

o 1916 - Yuan's sudden death sends Northern China into civil war, while Sun returns to take control of KMT government in South China.

o 1921 - <u>Communist Party</u> of China (CPC) formed. Early members include Mao Zedong, and Zhou Enlai. Deng Xiaoping joins as CPC Youth League member. At insistence of Soviet Union, CPC joins KMT to fight Northern warlords.

o   1925 - Sun Yatsen dies. Chiang Kaishek now in control of KMT.

o   1927 - After jointly defeating Northern warlords, CPC organizes a strike against Chiang and KMT. They are brutally suppressed; around 5,000 people are killed.

o   1931 - Japan invades Manchuria.

o   1934 - The Long March: Encircled and outnumbered, communists flee, marching c10,000km and crossing dozen mountain ranges. Many die, but they succeed in regrouping at new base in Yan'an, Sha'anxi.

o   1936 - Chiang famously said: *"The Japanese are a disease of the skin, the Communists are a disease of the heart"* and wanted to focus on defeating Communists first. His generals Zhang Xueliang and Yang Hucheng disagreed and kidnapped him, forcing him to agree to United Front with Communists against Japanese.

o   1937 - Sino-Japanese War starts.

o   1937-45 - United Front ends when Chiang stops distributing US arms to Communists. During war KMT retreat westwards to Chongqing as eventual war-time capital; while CPC retreat to countryside.

o   1945 - Japan surrenders in China war theatre.

o   1945–49 - By end of WWII KMT had bankrupted China while CPC had built strong, national following from rural bases. Est. civilian deaths - 10m and military - 1.3m.

o   1949 - Chinese Liberation Army takes Beijing and on October 1, 1949, Chairman Mao declares at Tiananmen Square foundation of the People's Republic of China defined constitutionally as a 'people's democratic dictatorship'.

{Mainly derived from: Beijing Made Easy: 20th Century Chinese History Timeline – www.tinyurl.com/co5s7qn}

2.4   India's Twentieth Century Timeline to mid-century

The first half of the 20th Century was troubled times for India too - escaping from colonialism to independence, and into the trauma of partition.

•   1855 - Congress Party formed, with initial impetus from Allan Octavian Hume.

•   1906 - Muslim League forms and splits from Congress.

- 1928 – Start of the <u>Civil Disobedience Movement</u> – Ahimsa (non violence, peaceful resistance) and Satyagraha (following the principles of truth) led by Mahatma Gandhi.
- 1939-45 - <u>WWII did not affect India</u> directly, although Indian soldiers played important roles as contingents in the British Army and won many gallantry awards including the Victoria Cross. Near the end of the war a Bengali independence fighter <u>Netaji Subhas Chandra Bose</u> joins the Japanese and invades British India, but is defeated easily.
- 1942 - Gandhi launches the <u>Quit India Movement.</u>
- 1947:
    - August 14, saw <u>birth of Pakistan,</u> an Islamic republic.
    - August 15, <u>India won its freedom,</u> ending c350 years of British presence and formed secular republic. Britain left India divided in two.
    - In aftermath of <u>partition</u> - devised under Lord Mountbatten - huge population exchange occurred between two countries. Around 14.5 million people crossed borders; half were Muslims moving to Pakistan from India while other half were Hindus and Sikhs moving other way.
    - Newly formed governments were completely unequipped to deal with migrations of such magnitude, and massive violence and slaughter occurred on both sides of borders. Estimates of number of deaths are around 500,000.
    - Whether partition of these countries was wise and whether it was done too soon is debatable. Even imposition of official borders has not stopped conflict between them. Border issues, left unresolved by British, have caused two wars and continuing strife between India and Pakistan; and with China.
- 1948, January 30: <u>Mahatma Gandhi assassinated</u> by Hindu extremist.
- 1950, January 26: Republic of India inaugurated. The constitution clearly defined India as a secular state with equality for all. Caste system, dowry system, and suttee - where widows threw themselves on their husband's funeral pyre - were outlawed.

{Mainly derived from: Kamat potpourri 20th Century India - http://tinyurl.com/bcab6ud }

2.5   Sixty years on from Liberation - 1949 to 2009

Turmoil in China mostly caused by the Great Helmsman, Chairman Mao; eventually resulting in a peaceful and prosperous China, Mao could only have dreamed of.

- 1949–1989 - Series of Five-Year Plans initially based on Soviet model of planned economy.
- 1949–1956 - Generally seen as the 'good years' of Chinese socialism. Land is redistributed to peasants and the economy grows.
- 1950-53 – Chinese People's Volunteers joins Korean War and enters North Korea in November 1950 as UN forces with South Korea repulsed North Korea's attempt to reunify country through arms almost to Chinese border along Yalu River. After series of see-saw battles, initially with Chinese and North Koreans pushing far south, truce was agreed that settled border along 38th parallel. China withdraws its Volunteers.
- 1956 – 'The Hundred Flowers' Campaign encouraged intellectuals to give their opinions about the government. Many that did were sent to jail in the anti-rightist purge that followed.
- 1956 - Brief war with Burma when Chinese forces invaded Burma, clashing with Burmese troops and taking disputed territory in northern Burma.
- 1958–60 – 'The Great Leap Forward', attempt to boost production through re-redistribution of land into communes and millions of backyard 'steel furnaces'. Apparently, Mao was told by some economists that a key measure of level of industrialization is iron and steel production. With so many communes and neighborhood communities at Party's beck and call, what better way to boost this indicator. Not surprisingly, the result was two failed harvests and millions of deaths from starvation.
- 1962 - China made several attempts to negotiate its border with India delineated by Sir Henry McMahon (of British Raj) agreed by Tibetan authorities, then a vassal state of Imperial China, but not accepted by China. India refused to negotiate. China was also highly irritated by India providing refuge to Dalai Lama since1959, supporting him, in effect, to set up government in exile. After repeated threats, Chinese tanks rolled over Himalayas into western Himalayan areas and Assam in the east and captured strategic oil

fields. Indian Army was totally unprepared as it thought Himalayas impassable for tanks. After several months of occupation, China unilaterally withdrew from Assam. It has however retained Aksai Chin in the west. India lost *'face'* in a big way. The <u>dispute has yet to be resolved</u>.

- 1966 - After few years away from power, Mao starts *'Great Proletarian Cultural Revolution'*. Cultural Revolution was time of utter chaos: students formed into bands of 'Red Guards' destroying anything representing the West, capitalism, religion or tradition. Mao's rivals within Party were purged, thousands of lives were ruined, layers of managers and professionals were sent to farms or mines - some never to return, health and education system collapsed, and much of China's cultural heritage was destroyed.

- 1969 - 2005 - Territorial dispute arising from nineteenth-century treaties imposed on China by Russia concentrated on boundary alignment along Amur and Ussuri Rivers. Beijing sought settlement on basis of compromise, and insisted on full renegotiation. Moscow refused to negotiate and used military force to impose treaties. China responded, and in <u>1969 clashes</u> on Ussuri River brought conflict to brink of war that could have involved tactical nuclear weapons. In 1986 Moscow broke deadlock by reversing its approach and agreeing to negotiate. By 2005 Sino-Russian boundary had been agreed and legitimized in new treaties.

- 1976 – The chaos of the Cultural Revolution ends with death of Mao. Mme Mao and her *'Gang of Four'* are arrested. Hua Guofeng takes over, but has no real power base.

- 1977 – Schools and universities re-open for business after 12 years of statis. Anyone could apply for the 273,000 university places. Nearly 6 million did, and only 4.7% gained places. But from that *class of '77* come the leaders, both political and industrial, of 21st Century China: including Li Keqiang, premier designate in 2012, Zhang Yimou, filmmaker (*Raise the Red Lantern*) and Chen Kaige (*Farewell my Concubine*).

- 1978 – <u>Deng Xiaoping</u> ousts Hua Guofeng and, for almost the first time in Chinese history – imperial or otherwise – allows his predecessor to retire in peace.

- 1979 – <u>China invades Vietnam</u> as response to what it considered to be collection of provocations and policies on Vietnam's part. These included Vietnamese intimacy with Soviet Union, <u>mistreatment of</u>

ethnic Chinese living in Vietnam (the Boat People), 'imperial aims' in Southeast Asia, and spurning of Beijing's attempt to repatriate disaffected ethnic Chinese in Vietnam to China. Strategically, some military analysts say this was carried out to demonstrate that the Soviet Union was powerless to intervene when one of its client states was attacked. But it does not win outright and withdraws after 29 days.

- 1980 – Deng begins policies of 'reform and opening up' which see China open up its economy and (initially) political life.
- 1989 – Violent suppression of Tiananmen Square protests by the PLA dents hopes for further political reform and tarnished China's international image.
- 1997 – Deng dies, Hong Kong returns to China. Economic reforms continue to accelerate.
- 2009 –October 1: China celebrates 60th anniversary of liberation. China is third after Japan in nominal GDP and number 1 in exports.

{Partly based on: Beijing made easy – Beijing history – 20th Century Chinese History Timeline - http://tinyurl.com/bcab6ud }

2.6   Sixty years on from Independence - 1947 to 2007

Two more assassinations in India, both in the same dynastic Gandhi family (though unrelated to the Mahatma); eventually resulting in relative stability and prosperity.

- 1947-1990 - Series of Five-Year Plans loosely based on Soviet model of planned economy.
- 1947-49 – 1st Indo-Pakistani War.
- 1949 – India was 15th country to recognize the People's Republic of China.
- 1956 – Chinese Premier Zhou Enlai visits India and *Hindi-Chini bhai-bhai* slogan was coined, which means *"Indians and Chinese are brothers"*; and agreed the Panch Sheel (5 principles) of co-existence.
- 1959 – His Holiness the Dalai Lama escapes to India from Tibet.
- 1962 – Indo-Chinese War started by China in frustration at lack of progress in settling border demarcation. To India's shame, Chinese living in the border areas affected by the war were detained at Deoli, Rajasthan a camp set up by the British for Japanese prisoners but not used until then. Also, India defined 'Chinese' as anyone with at least one grandparent of Chinese ethnic origin, similar to the

Nazi definition of a Jew! Even second and third generation migrants were treated as 'undesirable' aliens.

- 1964 – First Prime Minister Jawaharlal Nehru dies.
- 1965 – 2nd Indo-Pakistani War.
- 1966 – Prime Minister Lal Bahadur Shastri dies at Indo-Pakistan summit shortly after the peace treaty is signed; Indira Gandhi, daughter of Nehru no relative of the Mahatma, becomes PM.
- 1971 – 3rd Indo-Pakistani War which started as a civil war in East Pakistan which escalated and India got involved and ended with the creation of Bangladesh.
- 1972 - The Simla Agreement is signed between Indira Gandhi (daughter of the first premier Jawaharlal Nehru, a Kashmiri Brahmin living in Allahabad, who married Feroz Gandhi, a Parsi also from Allahabad, no relation to Mahatma Gandhi) and Zia A. Bhutto (who was later executed some say on false charges and father of Benazir Bhutto, who was later assassinated in her own country).
- 1975-77 - State of Emergency declared due to internal threats, mainly the rise of Sikh separatism.
- 1984 - *Operation Bluestar* launched against the separatist Sikhs hiding in the Golden Temple at Amritsar, subsequent assassination of Indira Gandhi, and violence against Sikhs.
- 1989 - National Congress Party loses general elections for first time.
- 1991 - Congress made comeback, but did not have mandate. Prime Minister P V Narismha Rao starts economic reforms. Rajiv Gandhi, son of Indira, is assassinated by female suicide bomber connected with Tamil Tigers of Sri Lanka.
- 1995 - The notorious Y2K (end of 20th century) software fix creates boom for Indian programmers. Start of Indian outsourcing.
- 1996 - National Congress Party loses again.
- 1999 – Kargill War between India and Pakistan.
- 2004 – National Congress Party regains power with decent majority and Dr Manmohan Singh appointed as Prime Minister. Economic reform now in earnest.
- 2007 August 15, India celebrates 60th anniversary of Independence.
- 2009 – National Congress Party retains power with large majority. Economic reform accelerates.

{Partly based on: Kamat's potpourri – India's 20th Century http://tinyurl.com/bcab6ud }

3 SOCIAL AND CULTURAL DIFFERENCES: CHINA'S SELF-CONTAINMENT AND INDIA'S BRITISH INFLUENCE

Everyone is influenced by one's past. So it is with nations. China had been conquered by foreign invaders several times. But unlike India, the conquerors adopted Chinese language, practices and culture. As a result, China has remained largely self-contained.

The pages to follow will cover:
o   China's self-containment and India's British influence
o   Chinese homogeneity versus Indian diversity
o   Different mindsets:
    o   Chinese mindset is practical, material and down-to-earth
    o   Indian mindset is philosophical, spiritual and transcendental.
o   Chinese and Indian variances in body, mind and spirit
o   Uncanny similarities too.

3.1   China has remained large self-contained

Despite sending its best and brightest abroad for further education since the beginning of the 20th Century - Sun Yatsen, Chou Enlai, Deng Xiaoping and many other leaders all went abroad as post-graduates - Chinese education is home grown. That is not to say it has not learnt from foreign methods and systems. For example, in Imperial times, civil service exams were mainly proving that one had learnt Confucius analects. Since then modern and different criteria apply.

Nevertheless, China has always and continues to believe in education and primary school is compulsory. Consequently, it has achieved relatively high literacy - 91%, especially amongst women - 87%; and it produces over 600,000 new engineering graduates and 530,000 science graduates each year. However, of these c300,000 engineers per year are of the requisite standard – see <u>Facts and Myths in the Globalization Debate</u>, esp slides 6 & 7.

Chinese **institutions** are mainly home-grown, though through quasi-colonial influence and, later, Soviet influence, some western practices have been adopted. But there are huge gaps and differences with western and global standards & practices such as in legal matters, rule of law, business institutions and practices such as treatment of <u>copyright and other intellectual property rights</u> and so forth; though reforms are continuing as China matures. In particular, there is no clear separation between the legislative, judiciary and executive branches of government. This last difference, of course, is more to do with being a single-party dictatorship rather than not recognizing and adopting best practice elsewhere.

One reads about **copyright infringements**, counterfeit and fake products in China. The story that takes top prize is the publication (this time in Taiwan rather than China) of a Chinese translation of a book entitled *Steve Jobs' 11 Pieces of Advice for Young People* by John Cage. It contains 11 pearls of wisdom. But nowhere can one locate the original English language version nor can John Cage be traced. This must surely be the fake amongst fakes which mimics no original apart from the concept. However, as China starts to develop its own brands, it is beginning to take copyright and IPR more seriously.

China has **developed economically** above all expectations over the last 30 years. As some economists noted, never in human history has a nation lifted itself out of dire poverty in a single generation:

o   Nearly 50% live in *towns*, and there are 160 cities > 1m population.
o   It has developed a *middle class* (variously defined as either earning >$10k pa or between $6k and $30k pa.) of 200m growing to 500m by 2020, who save $150bn per year (over 15% of income) but they are now also spending.
o   In 2009 Beijing had an estimated vacancy for 500,000 household maids of which there was a 100,000 shortfall. This isn't due to lack of applicants, but due to their lack of knowledge of big-city customs.

o   It has developed *home ownership* from 0 to 70% in 20 years. Britain has a similar percentage.

o   It has a million $ *millionaires* and over 200 $ billionaires practicing conspicuous consumption – according to Huran, a Shanghai publication. Outside of US, China is no 2 for Rolls Royce, Mercedes and BMW. Over 1/3 of bidders at auctions of Chinese antiques held by Sotheby's and Christie's are Chinese and rising.

o   It offers *cheap labor*, but wages are increasing – with mandated increases in minimum wages of around 10%. But for the recent (2008) recession, China would have been short of young workers.

o   The *ultra poor* (<$1.00 per day) comprises 10% of population. For decades it tries to practice a policy of *'No peasant left behind'*.

o   Mao was quoted as saying: *"women hold up half the sky"* to emphasize the fact that women should be treated equally under communism. According to the <u>Sunday Times Magazine</u>, May 22, 2010, a third of Chinese millionaires are women (and not by inheritance, yet); 8 out of 10 Chinese companies have senior women execs, and 60% of business school graduates are women. This is not surprising, as 82% of Chinese women have mothers who work (or worked) for a living.

o   It has eliminated many *slums* but many remain which are gradually being replaced by affordable high-rise apartments. In 2006 there were more slum dwellers in China than India. But the situation has reversed.

o   In 2007, Premier Wen Jiabao said at the World Economic Forum in Dalian, north eastern China that despite the large national GDP, *China was still a poor, developing country*. He said: if you divide a large number (national GDP) by another very large number (the population) you get a small number. He was referring to the per capita GDP.

3.2   India's British influence

Whilst China has remained largely self-contained despite its history of many foreign invasions, India is quite different. India's conquerors tended not to adopt Indian language, practices and culture, resulting in massive diversity - more of that later. And, in particular, its British colonial legacy, in particular the English language as well as many of the institutions such as parliament, democracy and corporate governance and so forth, has been embedded into India and have stood it in good stead.

India is more 'western' after years of colonial legacy

Some analysts would say that Britain bequeathed India with: English language, secular law, education system, constitutional government, government bureaucracy and the railways.

Most secondary schools in the upper tier conduct lessons in English. Many of these were established by Christian missions during the Raj for both British kids and those of aristocratic, wealthy or well-connected Indians. Over time they opened to middle class families and now often to poor kids who pass tough entrance exams. Many are run in English public school style, with cricket, soccer, hockey and perhaps boxing as main sports; and blazers and striped ties in winter for boys. More importantly, as English is the medium of instruction, Shakespeare and other classical English literature are on the curriculum and so graduates can speak English as well as any English kids, though sometimes a bit archaically. In fact, some of these Indians not only think but also dream in English.

Many who live in Commonwealth countries will know, *mission schools* are prevalent and often amongst the top performing. And they were so in China. My paternal grandfather went to St Xavier's a Jesuit run school in Shanghai. Years later, I studied at St Xavier's, Calcutta.

For kids determined to succeed, often entrance to one of the elite Indian Institutes of Technology (*IIT*) is sought after. Competition is fierce - 60 candidates for each place. Some IIT graduates had moved abroad, with many staying on as professors and others ending up as entrepreneurs, such as in Silicon Valley. The majority remains in India and usually is very successful in industry or commerce, though some, like Jairam Ramesh entered politics very successfully.

What else can we say about Indians?
- Indians are generally more *fluent in English* than the Chinese. And more Indians speak English than Chinese do.
- But India has lower literacy than China: 60% (45% women). Worse for Dalits (‚outcastes'): 31% for men and 11% for women. Lack of educated workers is beginning to hamper economic growth.

- It produces over 250,000 new _engineering graduates_ and nearly 700,000 _science_ and _math_ graduates each year. However, note should be taken of the reality behind the headline figures. There are probably around 100,000 engineering graduates per year of requisite standard - see Facts and Myths in the Globalization Debate, esp slides 6 and 7.
- Indian _institutions_ are largely based on _19th Century British institutions_ adapted to Indian conditions and updated at the time of independence. For example, there is clear separation between the legislative, judiciary and executive branches of government. The civil service is modeled on that of British India. And the Bombay stock exchange was modeled on the London one and opened in 1850s, the oldest in Asia, and company laws were originally derived from British company laws. At one time, Indian lawyers and judges dressed similarly to British counterparts and the barrister would address the judge as _"milord"_.
- They often dwell as large _'joint' families_.
- India has over 150,000 $_millionaires_ and c100m _middle class_ people.
- It has more _'ultra' poor_ (<$1 per day) than China: 30% of population.
- _Slums_ exist in large cities - one estimate says slum population doubled in last two decades, though there are plans to replace them by affordable high-rise apartments over next decade. Between £500m to £1bn promised for Bombay in _Vision 2020_. But it is not clear how 'industries' such as plastic recycling and clay pottery now run in places like Dharavi with 85% employment - made famous by _Slumdog Millionaire_ - will be accommodated.
- There is also less _opportunity for women_, despite being granted full suffrage in the constitution in 1949, especially in lower-level jobs. In addition, traditional 'son is better than daughters' attitude, just as in China, made worse by a dowry system, officially outlawed, is still practiced, especially in rural areas.
- Nevertheless Indira Gandhi was Premier for many years. In 2009 Pratibha Patil was elected as its first woman President and Meira Kumar as its first woman Speaker. Also, a January 2010 New York Times news item says that HSBC, JPMorgan Chase, Royal Bank of Scotland, UBS and Fidelity International in India are run by women. Before you say: _"Ah, but they are all non-Indian companies"_, the CEO of Indian banks ICICI and Axis are women, and half of the deputy governors at the Reserve Bank of India are women. Even more

29

encouraging is legislation first proposed in 1996 to reserve 1/3 of seats in both the lower house and state assemblies for women is now showing signs of being passed.

3.3 China is homogeneous

Despite China's vast size and population, China is surprisingly homogeneous; because it has been largely isolated from the rest of the world - mountains to the east and south, oceans to the west and the wilds of Siberia to the north.

This section will cover China's homogeneity and the next will cover India's diversity.

China is homogenous and is made up of:

o   *Population* of >1.3 billion, growing at 0.6% and slowing; mainly due to the <u>one-child policy</u>, even though it applies to 2/3 of the total population. This is a worry and a concern that China will "*grow old before it gets rich*".

o   <u>*Males outnumber females*</u> to such an extent that kidnapping of young girls by families with a boy in order to have a ready-made bride when she grows up is becoming an issue in some rural areas. This imbalance is due to the combination of an ancient desire to have sons rather than daughters and the one-child policy. This policy is being relaxed but a demographic time bomb has already been lit.

o   *Ethnic groups* and *languages*: 92% Han, with 55 ethnic minorities, each with its own language. The main ones being Tibetan, Mongolian and Uighur; and a written language *Mandarin* as labeled in the West is readable by all though some in the more remote provinces speak dialects that have a remote resemblance to Mandarin. Manchu has more or less disappeared and absorbed.

o   *Chinese language* - commonly called *Mandarin*, but actually termed *Zhongwen* (language of the middle kingdom) or *Hanyu* (or Han language) from which is derived the Japanese term <u>*Kanji*</u>, meaning 'Han words' - is a nearly unique pictogram language. There is no alphabet, although the government is trying very hard to introduce <u>*Pinyin*</u>, a phonetic version based on Roman characters. If two Chinese from different regions find they cannot understand what the other is saying, they resort to finger writing the words on the palms of their hands.

o   But most urban and some rural kids now learn English as the international language of trade and communications - not least caused by IT being mostly English-based. One author, Ted Fishman, says that as many Chinese spoke English as a second language as there are English speakers in the US, Canada and UK combined.

o   _Religions_: mostly atheist, only 30% consider themselves to be religious. 200m are Taoist-Buddhist, 65m are registered Christians and c20m are Muslims.

o   Most of the Muslims are Hui's (who are ethnic Chinese, converted around the 1300 CE, many with the surname _Ma_ apparently Chinese shorthand for Mohammed) and Uighur's who migrated from the Altai Mountains around 800 CE onwards. The latter mostly live in Xinjiang (new province), formally designated in 1884.

o   Interestingly, just as foreign invaders who conquered China sooner rather than later were assimilated, so also foreign originated religions. Buddhism acquired quite a different nature and several local deities (e.g. Kwan Yin), although the Buddha was assiduous in not invoking divine powers in seeking enlightenment and his sutras on how to achieve a better future now or in some future incarnation can be summarized by: _"You are the sole arbiter of your own destiny."_

Talking of **Chinese names**, there are around 100 common surnames and, apart from possibly _Ma_, there is no religious or regional clustering. The colloquial for 'the public' is _lao bai xing_, which literally means "old hundred surnames".

Traditionally the second name is the 'generation' name where siblings would all have the same second name. The third name is the personal name. In places like Singapore and Hong Kong, sometimes married women would keep their maiden name along with the husband's surname, making it four names.

In modern China, the middle generation name is either not followed or sometimes dropped. This causes huge problems for the authorities as, it is not uncommon, at roll call in school, several kids would answer - for example - to _Wang Ta_ (= Wang senior). The authorities are encouraging parents to revert to a middle name when naming their children.

3.4   India is diverse

The previous section explored China's homogeneity. In this section, India's diversity is examined. Although India is also protected by water along the south west, south and south east and by mountains to the east and north, the west has several highly vulnerable passes, the Khyber Pass being the best known, through which invader after invader has entered India and in the process diversified it. India (together with

Pakistan and Bangladesh) is more like Europe than China. No wonder it is sometimes called the Sub-continent.

India is a land of 'unity in diversity'... so postulated the late Pandit Jawaharlal Nehru, first Prime Minister of India, in *Discovery of India* written during his imprisonment in the Fort at Ahmednagar by the British for his role in fighting for independence in 1942-1946.

Unity is still holding 60 years after independence. However, over these years, some 15 new states have been formed now totally 29 plus 6 union territories. Some were recognition of areas with unique ethnic groups such as Nagaland in Assam; others were incorporation of extra territory such as Goa and Sikkim who decided it had no future as a small land-locked resource-poor country. But most were due to ethnic, linguistic or religious disharmony, such as Haryana, mainly Hindu and Hindi-speaking split from Punjab, now mostly Sikh and Punjabi-based and in 2009; and Telangana is being formed out of Andhra Pradesh.

Diversity is certainly there. India has:
* A *population* of c1.2 billion growing at 2.1% and slowing along the pattern seen all over the world as a society becomes affluent and infant mortality drops. But the people comprises of:
* *Ethnic groups*: Indo-Aryan 72%, Dravidian 25%, Mongoloid and other 3% (CIA World Factbook). Consequently, surnames are a very good indicator of religious or ethnic origin and, sometimes, of caste as well.
* *Languages*: 18 official: Hindi 41%, Urdu 15%, Bengali 8.1%, Telugu 7.2%, Marathi 7% plus 1,650 dialects. Such is the diversity that often two educated Indians from different ethnic backgrounds find it easier to converse in English. English is one of the official languages and is accepted as an alternative to Hindi in parliament and for central government reports and forms (of which, unfortunately there are many.)
* *Religions*: Hindu 80.5%, Muslim 13.4%, Christian 2.3%, Sikh 1.9%, Buddhist 0.8%, Jain 0.4%. India has the third largest Muslim population after Indonesia and Pakistan. Incidentally, the origin of Kerala Christians dates back to 52 CE, when St. Thomas the Doubter landed near Cochin. He visited different parts of Kerala and converted local inhabitants. Not surprisingly, many male Keralan

Christians are called Thomas. This assertion means that Keralan Christianity pre-dates all European Christianity.

- India also has a rigid 3,000 year old _Hindu caste system_, outlawed since independence, but still much in evidence 60 years later:
  - There are four Hindu castes and then there are the 'outcasts', the Dalits or 'untouchables' >150m (16%population).
  - Including other lower castes and ethnic minority tribes they form nearly 50% of India's population! Premier Manmohan Singh said that this is India's 'apartheid'.
  - But affirmative action is very strong for education and government posts and elected positions; nearly 30% of places are reserved and creates resentment in higher castes.
  - In 2007, tens of thousands of Gujjars - traditionally herdsmen rioted in Rajasthan - when the promise to be officially demoted in caste terms and hence could enjoy positive discrimination did not happen.
  - Nevertheless, the first Indian Vice President Dr B R Ambedkar who developed constitution was a Dalit. And a lady Dalit, Mayawati Kumari, currently chief minister of Uttar Pradesh (India's most populous state), was contending to lead the country.
  - The good news is that with the affirmative program, increasing education and - more importantly - the desire to educate one's kids whatever the cost, and IT (see later page), things are looking up for women, the poor and the Dalits.
  - It should be noted that caste is practiced not only by Hindus but also by Sikhs (though slightly less rigidly) and also by Muslims (both in India and Pakistan, particularly in the Punjab) and some Indian Christian communities.

You need no further demonstration of India's diversity than considering that when Sonia Gandhi stood down as PM-in-waiting when Congress won in 2004, we had the unlikely situation of an Italian Catholic woman giving way to a Sikh swearing the oath of allegiance to a Muslim President in a Hindu-majority nation.

For a contemporary view of India's diversity, read: _India's Unending Journey - Finding Balance in a Time of Change_ by broadcaster, Sir Mark Tully.

3.5   Chinese and Indians have very different mindsets

In addition to the influence of history and geography, Chinese and Indians are intrinsically very different. One observer feels they represent humanity's opposite poles. But they also share many common cultural and behavioral traits.

Three key differences in mindset

Sun Shuyun's book _Ten Thousand Miles without a Cloud,_ is a beautifully written account of her journey retracing the steps of one of the most popular figures in Chinese history, the seventh century monk Xuanzang. He crossed over a hundred kingdoms including today's Afghanistan in eighteen years to reach India via the Khyber Pass searching for true Buddhism. He was deeply concerned that the Buddhism practiced in China, which reached it in the second century BCE in the time of Asoka, had been misinterpreted and corrupted. On his return he brought true Buddhism to China, from whence it reached Japan and gave rise to Zen Buddhism.

Shuyun recounts a discussion she had with an Indian archaeologist, _Dr Agrawal_ of the Archaeological Society of India. He felt that people talk about differences between East and West, but in his view _"China and India seem to be humanity's polar opposites"_. In his view there were three differences between Chinese and Indians.

Chinese are:
o   Practical, with a 'can do' attitude
o   Materialistic
o   Down to earth – 'both feet on the ground'.

For Chinese, the world we live in is all there is.

Indians, by contrast, are:
o   Philosophical, the need to find 'meaning'
o   Spiritual
o   Transcendental – 'head in the clouds, feet on the ground'.

For Indians, religion dominates daily life; and this life is but one of many reincarnations.

3.6 Chinese are practical, materialistic and down to earth

Practical

The Chinese are both practical and pragmatic, which includes the ability to live with contradictions. This enables China to accept the handover of Hong Kong with the principle of 'one country, two (incompatible) systems'? Or that China regards Taiwan as a renegade province, yet bilateral trade between them is nearly double that of China with India and half that between China and the US; and Taiwanese FDI: foreign direct investment in China is only exceeded by that of US and Japan. China claims to be a 'socialist system with Chinese characteristics'. One can argue that it is a 'capitalist system with Chinese characteristics'!

Materialistic

Chinese materialism is self-evident in the way Taiwan first and then China - once the barriers were lifted - became world leaders in all kinds of industries. It is also evident on the Mainland where despite legislation and central government efforts to curb pollution often by illegal industrial firms, local authorities look the other way in order to encourage production and expand the local economy and so of the 20 most seriously polluted cities in the world, 16 are found in China. 40% of Chinese rivers are polluted.

Down to earth

Chinese down to earth (unpretentious or affected; straightforward) style is evident in the way Chinese live away from the main urban centres. But even in 'sophisticated' Hong Kong, Shanghai and Beijing, Chinese (whose metabolism doesn't really gel with alcohol), will dilute expensive wine and cognac with Coca Cola without regard of how it would look to westerners.

One of the best books on Chinese culture sprinkled with bits of relevant history and economics that illustrates this trait is _China Road_ by Rob Gifford a journalist who lived in China for many years and speaks fluent Mandarin. His book is about a 3.000 mile journey he made from

Shanghai to Urumqi, the capital of Xinjiang, much in the news in the summer of 2009 with unrest amongst the Uyghur Muslim minority, just before moving back to the West.

An example to illustrate the Chinese mindset

Elsewhere we explain the imbalance between number of men and women caused by the preference for sons exacerbated by the one-child policy and the availability of abortions. So we have more men than women in China. If that is not enough of an issue for eligible bachelors seeking brides, according to the New York Time, 15/04/2011, the practical, materialistic and down-to-earth attitude of Chinese women means that <u>unless the man owns a flat</u> or, at least, earns enough to be able to own a flat, he may as well resign himself to a single life. Some women go as far as asking that as one of the key questions on the first date. As one said: *"It's the guy's responsibility to tell a girl right away whether he owns a flat or not. It gives her a chance not to fall in love."*

Example of Chinese practicality

As a Chinese living in a Chinese community in Calcutta, I saw the practical attitude of the Chinese. In the 1950s, imported British chocolates in tins were an expensive luxury item. But for 'face' sake you had to give this kind of present to people you visited. However, the receiver would not open the tin and 'waste' it. Rather she would keep it as a present for a later visit.

My Mum (and her Chinese lady friends) would keep a note of which expensive presents she had received from which of her friends, so she did not commit the ultimate faux pas of giving that very same gift back on her revisit.

The Four Books

It will be grossly incomplete not to mention that the Chinese mentality has historically been influenced by The Four Books.

The Four Books refer to *The Analects of Confucius* (*Lùn Yǔ*), *The Mencius* (*Mèng Zǐ*), *The Great Learning* (*Dà Xué*) and *The Doctrine of the Golden Mean* (*Zhōng Yóng*).

The former two are collections of sayings and teachings of Confucius and Mencius as well as sayings of their disciples while the latter two are chapters in *The Classic of Rites* (*Lǐ Jì*). Chu Hsi, a famous scholar of the Southern Song Dynasty, held that The Four Books together outlined the basic system of Confucian thoughts and constituted a better introduction to the complicated materials in the Classics, thus selecting these four texts from Classics and put them together as the Four Books.

The Four Books is an abbreviation for 'The Books of the Four Philosophers' because The Analects of Confucius, The Mencius, The Doctrine of the Golden Mean and The Great Learning are respectively attributed to four great Confucian philosophers, namely Confucius, Mencius, K'ung Chi (the grandson of Confucius), Tsang Shan (a disciple of Confucius). In the Ming and Qing Dynasties the Four Books were made the core of the official curriculum for the imperial examination, which endowed them with the superior status in China.

From: Cultural China – Four Books and Five Classics - http://tinyurl.com/d644xao

---

3.7 Indians are philosophical, spiritual and transcendental

Philosophical

Having lived in Calcutta, West Bengal for many years, I personally experienced the philosophical nature of Indians - be aware that the Bengalis are regarded as highly philosophical and intellectual by other Indians. Rabindranath Tagore, poet, philosopher and Nobel Prize winner 1913, is their folk hero, even today. Unlike Bollywood films mostly produced in Bombay, Bengali films tend to be more intellectual and philosophical such as those by Satyajit Ray.

And the West Bengal Communist Party had been in charge for three decades, making it the world's longest-running democratically-elected communist government. (It got voted out in 2011.) Someone once said that the British Raj may have had a much harder time if the East India Company decided to set up in Bombay rather than Calcutta.

By the way Bombay was part of a dowry from Princess Braganza of Portugal when she married Charles II, along with Tangiers. It is not clear that the Marathas would have become loyal soldiers as the Bengal Sepoys and Lancers were - up until the Sepoy Mutiny (first Indian war of independence). Anyway, after the second and final Anglo-Sikh war, the Sikhs joined the (British) Indian Army and the Sikh Regiment fought for the British until the end of WWII and won many battle honours, including several Victoria Crosses.

In particular, Indians are interested in metaphysics the study of reality and being - the basis of all four religions that originated in India.

Spiritual

An example of the spiritual nature of Indians is the attendance of the Kumbh Mela. According to Wikipedia:

"The Purna (complete) Kumbh takes place at four places (Allahabad, Haridwar, Ujjain, and Nashik) after every twelve years, while the Ardh Kumbh Mela is celebrated every six years at Haridwar and Allahabad. Over 45 days beginning in January 2007, more than 17 million Hindu pilgrims took part in the Ardh Kumbh Mela at Allahabad, and on January 15, the most auspicious day of the festival of Makar Sankranti, more than 5 million participated.

"The Maha Kumbh Mela ('Great' Kumbh Mela) which comes after 12 Purna Kumbh Melas which is after every 144 years is also held at Allahabad. The 2001, it was attended by around 60 million people {larger than the population of Britain.} making it the largest gathering in the world."

Also, as shown on the pages on Body, mind and spirit, Indians are more religious than Chinese.

Transcendental

And the transcendental attitude of Indians is well illustrated by the combination of drive to build significant businesses with the need to pay homage to ancient customs such as consulting astrologers for the best day and time to open a new factory.

Interestingly, Indians are more open than Chinese and very warm. This has been so for a very long time. Consider a poem by the fourteenth century Indian poet Amir Khusro Dehlavi, a Muslim Sufi – who brought qawwali music into India - who wrote in Urdu, ancestry was Turkik, counted himself the luckiest man alive to have been born in India and to have India as his motherland. He wrote:

"How exhilarating is the atmosphere of India
There cannot be a better teacher than the way of life of its people.
If any foreigner comes by, he will have to ask for nothing
Because they treat him as their own,
Play an excellent host and win his heart,
And show him how to smile like a flower."

3.8   Chinese body, mind and spirit

Regardless of whether China is more practical, materialistic and down to earth than India or India is more philosophical, religious and transcendental than China, both have a long tradition of religions and philosophies.

Chinese religions, philosophies and healthcare

Just because the Chinese are materialistic and pragmatic does not mean they are not also interested in the spiritual.

The _Tao Te Ching_ begins _with:_

"The Way that can be spoken is not the eternal Way
The name that can be named is not the eternal name
The nameless is the origin of Heaven and Earth
The named is the mother of myriad things."

It is the text of Taoism which is more of a philosophy than a religion. As illustrated by the quotation Lao Tzu, the purported author of the Tao Te Ching, specifically talked about the ineffable nature of creation but never talked about deities. Another philosopher, Chuang Tzu is credited with:

"I was a sleep and dreamt I was a butterfly. But then I woke up and wondered if I was a butterfly dreaming that I was Chuang Tzu."

Nevertheless, the Chinese ended up deifying and absorbing all kinds of existing deities into the Tao pantheon. Confucianism is even more of a philosophy and code of conduct than a religion. The old Chinese civil service exams were based on understanding the _Analects_ attributed to Confucius (Kongzi). Many other SE Asian countries including Korea, Taiwan, Singapore and to a degree Japan seem to have adopted a Confucian outlook.

Again, the Chinese ended up deifying Confucius. There seems to be a need for people to believe in something they can visualize and an 'ineffable being' or, worse, a mere philosophy is not enough.

Two snippets to close:

o   The Chinese Communist Party (CPC) had for decades been anti-Confucius, seeing his works as backward and blaming his philosophy of convention and conservatism for holding China back. Since 2007, no more. The CPC gave its blessing honoring him on his

2,557th birthday. It was not lip service, as China has now opened c250 Confucius Institutes around the world including ten in the UK.

o   The best estimate of number of Christians is about 65m in the same region as registered CPC members (c85 million). In times gone by, some cynical Chinese would accuse Christian converts of being 'rice Christians', viz they converted to be fed by the missionaries. But no more. Now it is truly an act of faith to declare one's Christianity.

o   When interviewed, some young, affluent, new party members will admit privately that it is not dogma that made them join, but rather better prospects. The party makes efforts to enroll the top 1 to 5% of high school leavers and graduates. They believe that if the *crème de la crème* become members, the rest will follow in spirit if not in fact.

Treating body, mind and spirit a la Chinoise

Although the Chinese are not as religious as the Indians, they have *tai chi* and the related *chi kung*, a form of meditation not dissimilar to the Indian *pranayama*, special breathing technique to integrate body, mind and spirit. And of course there is *Kung Fu*.

For treating the body there are *acupuncture* and Chinese herbal medicine. The downside of some of the Chinese treatment is the suffering of animals, such as the brown bear for its bile; or endangered species, such as the tiger for its paws or other parts.

There is the *I Ching*, or Book of Changes, the most widely read of the five Chinese Classics. The book was written by the legendary Chinese Emperor Fu Hsi (2,953-2,838 BCE). It is possible that the I Ching originated from a prehistoric divination technique which dates back as far as 5,000 BCE. It is used to answer your questions and to predict the future.

Then there is *Feng Shui* - the art of geomancing where the alignment of a building or the doors, windows and furniture in a room will be good or bad for the occupants.

Many believe in numerology. So it was no accident that the Beijing Olympics opened at 8:08:08 p.m. CST on 08/08/08 - 8 being a lucky number, sounding like the word for prosperity. And 2009 turned out to be better for China than for most other countries. By the way 4 is extremely unlucky as it sounds like the word for death. So, never, ever, invite your Chinese friends to tea at 4pm on April 4th!

3.9   Indian body, mind and spirit

Regardless of whether China is more practical, materialistic and down to earth than India or India is more philosophical, religious and transcendental than China, both have a long tradition of religions and philosophies.

Indian religions, philosophies and healthcare

Of the religions practised in India Hinduism, Sikhism, Buddhism and Jainism originated there. Up to around the 7th century CE, Hinduism was not uniform and there were many conflicting sects and schools. Buddhism was gaining ground.

Adi Shankaracharya through meditation, study of the *Vedas* and the *Vedanta* and widespread discourse with proponents of various sects and schools, unified Hinduism and founded four monasteries. These have continued to today and the heads of each is entitled Shankaracharya. They are sort-of like the Archbishops of York and Canterbury in the Anglican Church, though there is no allegiance to the state as is the case in the Church of England. In fact, when India became independent, the constitution specifically defined India as a secular state.

Partly due to this consolidation and reform of Hinduism, Buddhism started to decline in India. Fortunately, through Asoka and his successors Buddhism had been spread to both the south east and the west of India, Buddhism thrives today in much of SE Asia. It was the western spread that reached Gandhara, then a Grecian remnant of Alexander's empire – in today's north-east Pakistan and southern Afghanistan - from where the Grecian-style of hair was adopted for statues of Buddha, with frizzled hair. The real Buddha was a monk with a clean-shaven head. Interestingly, the Buddha in his sermons did not preach about a deity. Despite that, today, although many Buddhists adhere to his original teaching, many more have turned him and some of his key disciples into heavenly beings.

Hinduism is both a religion and a philosophy. One of the best books about Hinduism is *The Hindu View of Life* by Dr S Radhakrishnan, one of India's greatest philosophers. He was a scholar and then professor at Oxford University and later was appointed President of India in 1962. One of the central beliefs of Hindus is *moksha* which is the idea of release or liberation of one's soul from the cycle of rebirth and the losing of one's self into the Self.

Another concept is *dharma which* refers to duties that have to be performed at different stages of one's life. These must be completed without a thought of possible rewards or benefits and should also be accomplished to the best of one's ability. They are responsible for the prevailing social order in the world.

All four Indian-originated religions subscribe to the belief in *karma* - put simply a law of cause and effect, a *'reap as you sow'* or *'every force has an equal and opposite reaction'*. The main distinguishing aspect of karma is that, with the belief in reincarnation, the effect may take place a few lifetimes later than the cause. Sometimes, karma is used as an excuse for one's misfortunes, blaming some past incarnation. If one does enough good deeds for long enough over several lifetimes then eventually one will achieve *nirvana* or enlightenment. And according to Buddhist teachings one will no longer have to come back into this karmic cycle of suffering.

Incidentally, India has nearly as many Muslims - 150m, as Pakistan - 160m.

Treating body, mind and spirit a l'Indien

In addition to being religious, Indians are also strong believers in meditation for the mind and spirit - of which *Transcendental Meditation* TM is the best known in the west after the Beatles followed the late Maharishi Mahesh Yogi to his ashram in Rishikesh. Though they later abandoned the practice. Each meditator is given a personal mantra.

Then there is *yoga* which in Sanskrit means to unite, the practice of which unites the body, mind and spirit. There are numerous forms and schools. One of the most popular forms in the west is Hatha Yoga with its various asanas or postures and pranayama breathing exercises.

And the *Kama Sutra* guide to a healthy and vigorous sex life, accompanied by the erotic carvings in the Khajuraho temples. According to research, the Kama Sutra was not a Vedic text but developed later, perhaps in the Gupta period (c350 BCE).

Palmistry and *astrology* are very popular and used for horoscopes. The latter is also used to pick auspicious dates and times for important domestic events like weddings, starting new jobs or moving homes, but also for public events: the opening of a new school, factory or dam.

Just because Indians are spiritual or intellectual does not mean they neglect the body. So there is _ayurveda_ the earliest school of medicine known to mankind, with the associated body-diet categories or doshas: _vata, pitta_ and _kapha._

3.10 Uncanny similarities in culture and behavior

Although it is dangerous to generalise about 2.5 billion people (in fact more when one includes Chinese and Indians living out of their homelands), but from personal experience, experiences of friends and colleagues, and published material, I can say with some confidence that there are spooky similarities between Chinese and Indians.

Chinese and Indians both:
- _Are hierarchical and deferential_ They do not like to go against people higher up the hierarchy, even if they know the 'superior' is wrong and is about to make a regrettable decision - something many western clients in IT projects outsourced to Indian (or Chinese) teams learn to their cost.
- They also don't like to say: _"No."_
- _When they nod_ (especially the Chinese) as you are saying something, such as at an important presentation, don't assume they are agreeing with you. They are probably just indicating that they had heard and think they've understood what you've said, but not necessarily agree with that.
- They _don't like to ask questions_, especially in meetings. Asking questions implies they didn't understand you. That in turn implies that either you weren't clear or that they are not clever enough to get it.
- They also tend to be _very literal_ when answering questions. No attempt is made to try and understand the 'real question' even if it is often quite obvious.

To illustrate **taking words literally,** I recount a personal experience many years ago (but my Indian and Chinese friends tell me things have not changed that much).

I was living at a university town that happened to be a stop for the Calcutta-Delhi Express. I was travelling to Delhi and got to the station slightly early. So I asked the clerk: *"When is the next scheduled train to Delhi?"* To which he replied: *"The next scheduled train is in 10 minutes."*

After about 20 minutes and with no sign of the Delhi Express, I went to the counter and said: *"I thought you told me the next scheduled train to Delhi was in 10 minutes, 20 minutes ago. What's happening?"* His reply was: *"That is correct. But the scheduled train had been cancelled last night. So the next train to arrive here for Delhi will not be for another three hours."*

He wasn't been awkward or intentionally misleading. I hadn't asked the right question and he was not trained or motivated to answer the question I should have asked. After all, he wasn't paid to second guess what a customer wants.

Incidentally, as of the end of March 2010, passengers will no longer be allowed to travel on the roofs on most Indian railways. By the way, India has the world's largest railway with 1.4 million employees (said to be the largest civilian employer in the world; and probably second largest only to the Chinese Army).

Another example of **taking words literally**

Lest you think the Indian railway clerk's responses in the anecdote in the left panel were due to his lowly status or lack of understanding of English, or that the Chinese are very different, let me tell you another story.

A friend of mine, a British expat, was the Asia-Pacific CIO of a major multinational based in Hong Kong. He supervised local IT managers across the region. They were all reasonably well paid and fluent in English. A major system upgrade was being installed in Taiwan. It was a critical system and a date was agreed for it to go live, a Monday. He was in constant touch by email and phone with his Taiwanese colleague and things were going very well. On the eve of the go-live Monday, he telephoned his colleague and asked: *"Have you finished all the tests and is the system all OK?"* To which the reply was: *"Sure, the tests are all done and the system is OK."*

To my friend's utter surprise and shock, the Taiwanese factory manager rang him on Monday at the crack of dawn to complain that things were mayhem as the new system was not working and the old one had been shut off. He immediately contacted his Taiwanese IT manager and asked for an explanation. The reply was: *"There has been a major power cut that caused major problems and hence we couldn't cut over."* And when asked how long that had been going on, expecting a reply like: since early this morning, the answer was: *"since Sunday afternoon."*

Once again, the 'superior' didn't ask the right question and the 'subordinate' was not going to second-guess.

- They tend to *follow conventions and traditions.* Less so in cities, especially in China. For example, arranged marriages using professional matchmakers are common in India and in Chinese rural communities and with some city folk. Girl babies are still regarded as not necessarily a happy occasion, again more in villages than in cities. Both follow traditional festivals. In China, most of these are secular, such as the Chinese New Year and the mid-Autumn moon cake festivals. In India, most are religious, *Holi* color water festival to welcome spring, the *Pujas* (when a major deity is venerated and at the end of the period is immersed in the Ganges to send the prayers to heaven) held after the monsoon, and *Diwali*, the New Year. In addition, major Muslim holy days are public holidays such as *Muharram* and *Id ul-Fitr*; as are Easter and Christmas. It is thought that India has the <u>most holidays of any country</u>.

- Are strongly *family- and clan-oriented*. This works its way through nepotism in both private and public affairs, often to the detriment of the common good.

- Work best through *connections/relationships* (*quan xi* in Chinese). It's an extreme case of the British 'old boys' network' - it's about 'who you know rather than what you know or what you are good at'.

- Are *color prejudiced*. Light-skinned girls find it easier to attract husbands and if a dowry is involved, her parents pay less. L'Oreal (*"you're worth it"*) has research centres in China and India developing extreme white face powder. This, apparently, is also sought after in many other South East Asian countries as well as Japan.

- Have *high levels of corruption*. According to Transparency International's 2012 <u>Corruption Perception Index</u>, China ranks 80th and India 94th (Somalia at 174 is the worst). Incidentally, the country perceived to be least corrupt is Denmark, with the Nordic countries, Singapore, Switzerland, Netherlands, Australia, New Zealand, Canada and Luxembourg occupying the other top 12 slots. The UK is number 17 and the US is 19.

However, the more westernised a Chinese or Indian is, the less he exhibits these archetypical behaviours. Someone born in the West and can hardly speak his parents' language is not culturally a Chinese or Indian.

A banana?

I go to Hong Kong from time to time. My friends there who have known me for a long while eventually told me that I was a *'banana'*. When I looked nonplussed, they explained that I was *'yellow on the outside, but white inside'*. Later, when I recounted this to a much westernised Indian friend, he started laughing. When he finally stopped, he said: *"Wow, we are more alike than I thought. When I last visited Calcutta my relatives who had never left India told me I was a 'coconut': brown on the outside, but white inside!"*

Please note that both terms 'banana' and 'coconut' are essentially derogatory.

Crucially, you need to know about Chinese *'face'*, which also applies to much of the rest of South East Asia. Some westerners equate this to respect or reputation or honor. *'Losing face'* is sort of like losing honor or even humiliation. But face is much more than that. I think the only way one can grasp face is to read something like the excellent real-life anecdote on the website: Life in the Fast Lane – China Revealed – Concept of Face - http://tinyurl.com/5oz9vh

4 ECONOMIC DIFFERENCES - POST *GLASNOST*

One of the defining aspects of China and India is that their economies are growing faster than any of the developed nations and indeed faster than that of other BRIC countries. This aspect makes understanding their economies key.

In 2001, Jim O'Neill of Goldman Sachs invented the acronym *BRIC* for Brazil, Russia, India and China to epitomize the fastest growing developing countries. He based his notion on the developing countries with large populations, land mass (and natural resources) and growth.

Whereas Brazil and Russia have see-sawed a little - in 1978 Brazil was number 9 in GDP, Russia was number 7, in 1991, Brazil was 10 and Russia 7, and in 2009, Brazil was 10 and Russia 13 - both China and India have moved steadily up the ranks. China has benefited from the end of the Cold War and glasnost, in the manner of changes to *The World is Flat* as explained by Tom Friedman. BTW - for the first time, the BRIC countries met at a summit in June 2009.

BRIC was extended to *BRICS* in 2010, the *S* equal South Africa.

In the decade since BRIC was invented, much has occurred economically in China and India. In this section, we cover the following economic aspects:

o   We start with a summary of the recent economic situation in China in 2011 and 2012.

o   We then go back to cover how China kick-started after the end of the Cultural Revolution.

- o Next, we summary of the economic situation in India in 2011 and 2012.
- o We go back to note how <u>India changed gears</u> with the leadership of the then Economics Minister, Dr Manmohan Singh, and now Prime Minister.
- o This is followed by a look at China's seeming <u>obsession with infrastructure</u>; and
- o It's realization that its rapid development is causing environmental damage. So it is '<u>greening</u>' as fast as it can.
- o Then follows a pair of pages:
  - o China's emphasis on <u>manufacturing</u> and
  - o India's on <u>services</u>.
- o A quick look at how increasing affluence is creating a <u>blossoming of consumerism</u> in both countries.
- o Closing with how <u>Information Technology</u> is being developed and being used in China and India.

4.1   Recent economic situation in China

China maintained its position as no 2 after the USA in GDP terms in 2011-12. But despite some economists' optimism, it turns out that the BRIC countries are not immune to the economic problems of developed nations and the economies are not decoupled. Chinese manufacturing and exports are down from a year ago and in some areas 100s of business owners have fled the country and left employees and suppliers unpaid. The final outcome for 2012 is 7.8% and for 2011 was a growth of 9.2% down from 2010 at 10.3%. China is aiming for 8.5% growth in 2013.

Central government is trying to use policy mechanisms to control two opposing forces: inflation and slowdown which some economists deem to be impossible. We saw in 2012 a veering from one set of polices to the other, much as has been happening since the global economic crisis of 2008. Having said all of the above, no economist is predicting a hard landing for China. And signs are that the economy is turning in late 2012 with several months of increasing manufacturing output.

Chinese investments overseas

Chinese firms, both state owned and private, continue to make a large number of overseas investments – not surprising given the $3 trillion plus forex reserves. The short list below includes some of the investments made during the first eight months of 2012. There were five kinds of investments (or JVs) - which are not mutually exclusive - in rough order of priority:

Natural resources: oil and gas (Sinopec, CNOOC and PetroChina have all been very active in several continents, including North America - Nexen, Canada), coal, steel, minerals (incl Australia's Sundance), even arable land (parts of Africa and South America) - which serve an obvious need.

Infrastructure and other tangibles: manufacturing plants (Putzmeister), oil refineries (INEOS' Grangemouth (Scotland) and Lavéra (France), utilities (Redes Energeticas Nacionais, Energias de Portugal, Thames Water; Brazilian electricity grid), office blocks (Canary Wharf, London), housing in the US; Spanish construction company; all sorts in parts of Africa and the Caribbean (sports stadium, holiday resorts, roads, ports, etc) - which are 'safer' than holdings of US or Euro bonds and provides relatively predictable yields; they often also provide technology transfer at no additional cost.

Technology: esp new and innovative (UK's Centre for Integrated Photonics); geothermal energy (Iceland); Saab (to Chinese-Swedish JV); Hawker light aircraft (US); A123 Battery (US) - which builds for the future.

Brands: especially luxury brands like yachts (Ferretti), high fashion (Cerruti, Sonia Rykiel), essentials (Weetabix, Putzmeister); soccer (inter Milan) - which reduces the outflow of currency and increases the inflow as the population gains affluence and demand for luxury goods continue to expand. But also other brands such as Saab.

Financial houses, esp owners/managers of funds (BlackRock) - which are not as 'safe' as resources and tangibles, but much safer that Euro and $ bonds.

4.2 China kick starts in 1978

China has benefited from the end of the Cold War and glasnost, in a sense the change to *The World is Flat* as explained by Tom Friedman. Chinese economic renaissance began with economic reforms started by Deng Xiaoping in 1978 soon after the end of the Cultural Revolution. China was number 17 in GDP terms then (India was number 18). China joined the WTO in December 2001. By the end of 2010 China was number 2 after US.

Deng Xiaoping, the leader who eventually succeeded Chairman Mao after the end of the Cultural Revolution, once said: *"It doesn't matter if a cat is black or white, so long as it catches mice."* which did him no favors with Mao. In fact, that was one of the reasons he was sent for political correction through hard labor. Anyway, once Deng came to power in 1978, he initiated four modernizations: agriculture, industry, national defense and science and technology. Foreign Direct Investment (FDI) was permitted in several Special Economic Zones (SEZ) along the coast.

GDP growth since then has varied between 6.5 and 12+%; est: 7.5 for 2013.

1989: that was a momentous year

1989 was a momentous year: the fall of Berlin Wall - good for the West and eventually also for most socialist states; and Tiananmen Square protest with armed response by the People's Liberation Army - bad for Chinese seeking some form of political freedom, but eventually good in speeding up economic reforms.

There was a major hiatus in China after the Tiananmen incident. It seemed all reform would stop. However, Deng undertook his now famous 'southern tour' and gave his blessing to economic reforms, implicitly halting social and political reforms. Even today, political reform is not on the agenda.

China grew 10 times from 1978: and became a centralised Market Economy.

Foreign Direct Investment (FDI) is very high, unlike India until recently. And so-called private sector accounts for 60% of GDP, similar to UK. But a large part of that is actually still under state ownership and, possibly, control.

4.3   Recent economic situation in India

India maintained its position as no 10 in GDP terms in 2011-12, though the GDP growth in 2012 of 5.4% was a bit disappointing. The target for 2013 is 5.7%, down from previous years' 6-7%.

It is improving in terms of both export and attracting FDI. It is likely to be able to maintain its growth and not drop back a few points as China, given that it is not as reliant on exports.

Regrettably, despite many moves to reduce restricted practices, the opening up of the retail food business has hit a snag and so Indians will continue to shop at small, local groceries and bazaars as they have done for generations for a bit longer and not enjoy the economies and variety that comes with big supermarkets. Some feel this is a small price to pay to enable the small retailers to continue to earn a living.

There were several major cases of corruption and investor gloom, falling rupee and a bad monsoon.

Also in 2012, India suffered its greatest electricity blackout that affected around half the country for several days. After a bumper harvest, it did not have sufficient storage for all the grain, so a fair percentage was left in the open air.

4.4 India changes gear in 1991

India has also benefited from the end of the Cold War and glasnost, in a sense the change to *The World is Flat* as explained by Tom Friedman. Indian reforms from a highly bureaucratic and centrally-planned system began with the second return to power of the National Congress Party in 1991and the appointment of Manmohan Singh as Prime Minister. India was number 16 in GDP then (China was number 11). India joined the WTO in January 1995. By the end of 2010 India was at number 10.

After six years in the wilderness (for second time after independence) National Congress Party won again in 1991. Sonia Gandhi was seen as the natural successor to her assassinated husband Rajiv and her assassinated mother-in-law Indira. But for the good of the country and having a deep grasp or *realpolitik,* she stepped aside for Dr Manmohan Singh to lead Congress, and take over the post of Finance Minister.

Prime Minister P V Narismha Rao started economic reforms, led by Manmohan Singh. Dr Singh graduated from Punjab University in Chandigarh. He later studied economics at Cambridge and Oxford Universities where he gained a PhD. Before taking up his Indian position he worked for the World Bank.

Peak growth since then has varied between 5.5 and 10+%.

2004: India in overdrive

Manmohan Singh took over as Prime Minister, when Congress won with a majority in 2004. India has lower economy than China and growing slower. Because of this delayed start some economists regard India as 'China 15 years ago' It is a deregulating Planned Economy, opening up numerous SEZs.

India is still growing, with continuing demand for raw materials and quality products and services. But cost of commodities, wages & inflation are rising. Property is booming. And fuel is increasing cost of transport.

India is increasing trade with Africa to gain commodities and political goodwill. But China is way ahead in value of investments, energy contracts and infrastructure projects.

4.5   China seems to be obsessed with infrastructure

Since Liberation in 1949, one slogan has stayed constant through all the turmoil and twists and turns, and that is 'reconstruction'. In truth, apart from industrialization in the north east under Japanese rule during the mid-30s to mid-40s, industrial plants were not a major investment throughout the first half of the 20th century. War spending absorbed most of the foreign aid, mainly from the US. So it was really construction without the 're' - a code word for industrialization.

With this focus, China was able to provide energy, transport and other infrastructure that enabled it to become the 'factory of the world'; China overtook America as the world's largest manufacturer.

Energy

China added 80GWatt of power in 2011 which is slightly lower than that of the entire UK capacity. BTW: an average nuclear power station generates around 1GWatt. China will surpass the US in energy generated by 2012, with over 1,000 GW. $45bn was spent in 2009 in upgrading the national electricity grid.

Constantly berated for being the source of pollution caused by old coal power stations, China is investing substantially in new coal power stations using *advanced supercritical clean coal technologies*. But it takes time to replace the old with the new when the economy is growing so fast.

China is also investing in *nuclear* power stations and *wind farms* as well as in *solar energy*. In 2011 China vaulted past Denmark, Germany, Spain and the US to become the world's largest maker of wind turbines. Vestas of Denmark has invested in their biggest wind turbine plant in China. China not only makes them but deploys them extensively. They are mainly deployed in the windy deserts to the west of China, but as producing ramps up, they will be exported as well. Some 60GW of wind power was in operation by the end of 2011.

China has also become a world leader in solar voltaic panels with both indigenous firms and foreign-owned plants. Not only are these good for the 'green' agenda but also for jobs. It is estimated that over 1 million workers were employed in manufacturing 'green' plant in 2008 and some 100.000 new 'green' manufacturing jobs are being added each year.

In addition to making solar voltaic panels, *solar heat collectors* that work by recirculating water warmed by exposure to the sun is being installed in a big way. Apart from taking shares in oil companies and signing contracts with various national oil companies, China is laying a 7,000km *pipeline to move gas* from Turkmenistan via Uzbekistan and Kazakhstan.

Hydroelectric is the second main energy source and renewable. China has the most hydroelectric capacity in the world. We have all heard, read or seen pictures or videos of the Three Gorges Dam along the Yangtze. It is generating around 15GWatts and will eventually generate 22.5GWatts. The reservoir is 600KM long which is about the distance from London to Aberdeen in north Scotland.

Apart from hydropower, Chinese plans for renewable energy to make up 8% of total energy by 2020, up from today's 5.5% - a major achievement when met.

Road and rail transport

There is the continuing expansion of transport. There are 85,000 km of expressways at the end of 2011 (originally targeted for end of 2015) of which over half are multi-lane 'super-highways' or expressways, with another 5,000 km under construction, second only to the US, but catching up fast.

This is closely followed by massive expansion of the railways to 91,000 km by the end of 2011, planned to expand to 120,000 km by the end of 2020. It is second to the US, again and ahead of India with 65,000 km but not expanding at the same rate as China. Of that, the 12th five-year plan aims to complete 45,000 km of high-speed track by the end of 2015. However, the collision between two high-speed passenger trains at Wenzhou in July 2011 has put a pause to the Chinese programme while investigations are underway to identify the root causes, be they technical or human. The recent arrest of the railway minister for corruption does not help either. Towards the end of 2012, construction has resumed.

Air transport

China announced at the China Civil Aviation Development (CAAC) Forum, May 2009 that it would set up a national public air transportation system over the next three to five years. CAAC will reinforce and improve Beijing, Shanghai and Guangzhou airports as national hubs. There will be one flight between the three hubs every 30 minutes; and 30 long-haul international flights will be opened. Meanwhile eight regional hubs will be set up, and every one or 1.5 hours there will one flight between the eight regional hubs and the three national hubs. Artery network construction of 12 airports in Hangzhou, Nanjing and other cities will also be completed, and flights should be arranged every 1.5 to two hours.

This national and regional hub and spoke approach has become necessary due to the intensity of flights currently crisscrossing the country in a 'random' fashion. China had around 2,500 civilian aircraft by the end of 2011. Airbus is predicting that is going to treble over the next 20 years. BTW - China is the top buyer of civilian aircraft and India is not far behind.

Sea transport

Let me not swamp you with more statistics. Suffice it to say that more container ships load and unload at Chinese ports than any other country in the world. Six of the world's 10 busiest container ports in 2012 are in China.

Water

China has a very uneven distribution of water. The south is well watered by the monsoon, with three main river systems supplied by the snows of the Himalayas and the Tibetan plateau. But the north is relatively dry with unreliable rivers and sand storms blowing from the Gobi desert to the west. As many school kids will know, the Yellow River is also known as the River of Sorrow, alternating with flooding and drought.

As long ago as Kublai Khan (and reported by Marco Polo) there was a Grand Canal to connect the rivers in the south to ones in the north. However, that was for transport rather than to balance water supply.

The late chairman Mao Zedong proposed the idea of the diversion project in 1952, to ease the growing water shortages in the cities of Beijing and Tianjin and the northern provinces of Hebei, Henan and Shandong. Fifty years later, after extensive research, planning and discussion, on August 23, 2002 the project was approved by the State Council (equivalent to parliament) and work began on the eastern route of the project in December, construction commencing on the central route a year later.

The South-to-North Water Diversion Project is the largest of its kind ever. It involves drawing water from southern rivers and supplying it to the dry north. When finished, the work will link China's four main rivers – the Yangtze, Yellow River, Huaihe and Haihe – and requires the construction of three diversion routes, stretching south-to-north across the eastern, central and western parts of the country.

Key data:
Eventual diverted volume: 44.8 billion cubic meters per year
- Eastern Route   14.8 billion cubic meters per year
- Central Route   13.0 billion cubic meters per year
- Western Route   17.0 billion cubic meters per year

Eventual diversion: 3,723 km est.
- Eastern Route   1,156 km
- Central Route   1,267 km
- Western Route   1,300 km est.

The complete project, planned completion 2050, is expected to cost $62bn – more than twice as much as the Three Gorges Dam. The Eastern Route, partly based on the Grand Canal of Kublai Khan will be operational in 2013.

There is longer-term concern about the gradual evaporation of glaciers in the Himalayas and the Tibetan plateau. This should be of great concern as the northern rivers in India have the same sources.

Telecoms

Again - not hitting you with any detailed statistics - there are more mobile phones in China (over 1 billion in 2012) and after the US, more Internet users than anywhere else. Land lines and broadband are also catching up.

In conclusion

Focusing on infrastructure investment is not unusual for a newly industrialised country. This was the case with Europe and the US c150 years ago.

What is surprising is that India, despite embracing central planning, has not invested in infrastructure anywhere approaching that of the Chinese.

As we will show elsewhere, India is only now awakening to the need to invest in infrastructure.

4.6   Greening of China

China is woefully aware of its status as the world's biggest carbon emitter. Its main defense is that in per capita terms it is still a modest emitter and that there should be two standards, one for developed and the other for developing nations:

Carbon emission 2011: 1 China, 2 US, 3 India, 10 UK

Per capita emission 2011: 1 US, 9 UK, 16 China, 20 India

Despite opinion that China contributed significantly to the failure of the recent Copenhagen climate change summit (others would argue it was the US that wrecked it. But that's another story. In any case there is strong <u>Chinese-US collaboration</u> on green issues and technology), it is not sitting on its hands.

BTW - if you remember China's collective memory of the <u>century of</u>

humiliation and being forced to sign unequal treaties, it will go some way to explain why it will not be coerced into any 'unfair' treaty, but needs to be persuaded that it is not unfair. Giving China a bad name only reminds it of the Ah Q story and makes it more resolute not to sign.

For an easy to read and assimilate book on the reality of pollution and the effects of industrialization in China, read *When a Billion Chinese Jump: How China will save Mankind - or destroy it*, which is written as a personal travelogue from 'Shangri-La' in Yunnan in the south to 'Xanadu' on the steppes of Inner Mongolia by environmental journalist, Jonathan Watt.

China knows what is wrong and is doing a lot about it

It carried out a national pollution census that took two years and 570,000 staff. It knows that of 20 most seriously polluted cities in the world, 16 are found in China. 70% of Chinese rivers are polluted to some degree. There are increasing cases of birth defects and increased illnesses due to pollution where industrialization or old coal-powered generators run.

It escaped a major loss of face when the Beijing Olympics were not as smog bound as some Cassandra's were predicting. Much of the pollution of China's water, soil and air has been caused by the desire of local governments to compete against other authorities and regions for natural resources and meet production targets. Corruption has also produced a flood of illegal, or semi-illegal, small-scale but highly-polluting plants being set up throughout the country.

Some local authorities are imposing draconian rules. For example, Beijing has restricted the total number of new car license plates to 240,000 for 2011. This is against an actual 720,000 new licenses in 2010. There are also restrictions on rush hour ban for non-Beijing registered vehicles and movement of cars to particular days of the week.

At the 17th Congress of CPC, October 2007, the next 5-10 year objectives were:
1. Economy: Shifting economic growth from speed to quality.
2. Development: Developing scientific, sustainable and people-oriented approach to development.
3. Energy & environment: Improving energy and environmental conservation: resource efficient, environment friendly and renewable.
4. Global relationships: Harmonious development in the world

context.

Objective 3 is largely about the environment.

In 2009, China updated its national plan to further cope with the issue of climate change. Despite not signing any international agreement, China has set itself very ambitious targets in terms of CO2 emission, and per capita carbon footprint. China has official anti-pollution targets at national, provincial and regional level in place since 2007.

According to the Economist (The World in 2011) China has dedicated $220bn in 2009/10 to renewable energy. A generous subsidy will help sales of low-polluting cars in 13 big cities and large solar-power projects will get a 50-70% subsidy. Beijing already has several measures to reduce private car traffic. In September 2011 it is considering introducing congestion charges (like London). Greenpeace China is one of the largest NGOs in China and is seen to be an ally rather than an opponent (as it is in many other countries).

The 12th five-year plan (2011-2015) outlines major initiatives regarding the environment:

- Energy efficiency and environment services to be priority industries for the first time.
- 3tr Yuan for environment protection (twice previous period)
- Carbon intensity target to be set (sort of national carbon footprint)
- Environment tax on heavy polluters
- Mandatory carbon trading at regional level
- Other measures such as shift away from GDP-based performance evaluation.

Energy

On the infrastructure page we have already covered most of the advances being made to reduce old-technology coal-fired electricity generation that not only spew out enormous amounts of carbon dioxide but also contribute to acid rain and replace it by either high-technology coal-plants or renewables such as nuclear, hydroelectric, wind, solar power. Although China has only 15 nuclear plants (2012), 24 are under construction. In August 2011, China and the US signed an agreement to share joint research on clean coal power technology, which is only just as they are not only the two largest producers of CO2 but also with the highest increases in 2010. In the meantime, Russia is investing in new hydroelectric power plants in Eastern Siberia for export to China, while China is upgrading its national grid to the tune of $250 billion over several years. By 2020, China plans to have over 500GW of renewable power, up from 250GW, a doubling in a decade.

In January 2012, it announced a new offshore wind farm to be installed that will provide 300 MWatts; this will be expanded to 5 GWatts (the equivalent of 5 nuclear stations) by 2015. By then the total wind generated capacity will be 100 GWatts.

---

*Example of **solar energy** use*

Extract from - Renewable World Energy.com:
"Buildings in Rizhao, a coastal city of nearly three million on the Shandong Peninsula in northern China, have a common yet unique appearance: most rooftops and walls are covered with small panels. They are solar heat collectors.

"A combination of regulations and public education spurred the broad adoption of solar heaters. The city mandates all new buildings to incorporate solar panels, and it oversees the construction process to ensure proper installation. To raise awareness, the city held open seminars and ran public advertising on television.

"In Rizhao City, which means City of Sunshine in Chinese, 99 percent of households in the central districts use solar water heaters, and most traffic signals, street and park lights are powered by photovoltaic (PV) solar cells. In the suburbs and villages, more than 30 percent of households use solar water heaters, and over 6,000 households have solar cooking facilities. More than 60,000 greenhouses are heated by solar panels, reducing overhead costs for farmers in nearby areas.

"In total, the city has over a half-million square meters of solar water heating panels, the equivalent of about 0.5 megawatts of electric water heaters.

"The fact that Rizhao is a small, ordinary Chinese city with per capita incomes even lower than in most other cities in the region makes the story even more remarkable. The achievement was the result of an unusual convergence of three key factors: a government policy that encourages solar energy use and financially supports research and development, local solar panel industries that seized the opportunity and improved their products, and the strong political will of the city's leadership to adopt it."

Water

China is monitoring the status of glaciers on the Tibetan plateau. Apparently not long ago there were over 4,000 lakes, now they are down to 3,000.

There is a whole raft of central government legislation regarding the treatment of water from manufacturing and chemical plants. Western environmental companies such as Veolia and Purac are big in China.

Factories will install water treatment plants when forced to. But, according to some investigators, as soon as attention moves elsewhere, the owners will turn the treatment plants off saving electricity with local officials not only turning a blind eye but warning them if they hear a central government inspector is on the way.

Nevertheless progress is being made. Not least through people power. Increasingly, the public is raising protest and inviting journalists from Beijing to see for themselves. The Internet, especially the Chinese microblog site Weibo, also helps in that concerned citizens will raise alerts that environmental activists will track and often take up with central government departments. <u>Hefty fines</u> are imposed when culprits are found. But sometimes these are less than the cost of either installing or running the treatment plants.

Air

Any visitor to any of the big cities in China will have noticed the smog that hangs over the landscape sometimes obscuring the top of the many skyscrapers. However, China now has tougher legislation regarding car exhausts than anyone else including California.

<u>China has planted more trees</u> than any other nation. The World Bank data shows that China increased the extent of forest coverage between 1990 and 2010 (and has done even more since then) from 16.85% to 22.18%, while India increased its forests by only 0.47%. This increase nearly offset Brazil's reduction. The "<u>Green Wall of China</u>", an attempt to limit the expansion of the <u>Gobi Desert</u> is planned to be 2,800 miles (4,500 km) long and to be completed in 2050.

Nevertheless, China's forest coverage is only 61.5 percent of the international average and its per capita forest area only 25 percent. But since then a few more million trees have been planted, averaging 1 million pa or around 4m hectares pa. BTW - Brazil is losing 3m hectares of forest pa. Some cynics say that the Chinese army plant a lot of trees and with 2.5m soldiers, one per soldier is a large number. Be that as it may, a tree is a tree whether planted by a soldier or a civilian. In fact, since 1981 every citizen is required to plant at least 3 trees pa. High school graduates celebrate by planting a tree.

Recycling

As Western consumers know, much of our waste that does not go into landfills end up in places like China to be recycled. In fact, many of the container ships that deliver clothing, toys, and electronic appliances to western ports return laden with containers full of rubbish.

In this age of scary headlines about disappearing Arctic polar caps and climate change, it's reassuring to see the two richest business people in China are both in environmentally-friendly businesses. One is electric car battery and electric car tycoon _Wang Chuanfu_, born into a farming family, as one of the richest men in China. He has a 5.1 billion dollar fortune. His company BYD Co has Warren Buffett as one if it's more famous investors. Another is paper recycling queen _Zhang In_, whose Nine Dragons paper recycling firm imports recycled paper and sends it back as packaging for exports.

China is also the world's leader in producing plastic carrier bags. However there is a worldwide campaign to reduce their usage. But you can be sure the Chinese will think of some other way to recycle and reuse plastic.

In conclusion

China is very aware that it is a major source of pollution. The leadership had deemed it was a necessary evil. But as this section shows, it is now trying to make amends and is spending a vast amount to compensate. By contrast, even though India is also aware it is a major source of pollution, it has not reached a stage of development where it has surplus funds to do much about it, even if it had the will.

Note that many of the 'green' technology require the use of rare earths. China has a near monopoly of these minerals, though large deposits have been found elsewhere such as Greenland and Kazakhstan. And other countries with known deposits are beginning (or restarting) mining operations.

4.7 China has focused on manufacturing until recent years

There is a persistent view that China is focused on manufacturing and India on services. This may have been so 10-15 years ago. But today, both countries are moving into each other's 'specialties'.

As more and more western firms moved their production facilities to China to take advantage of the *'China price'* helped by preferential treatment in the Special Enterprise Zones, China has become the factory of the world. Initially they made low-priced consumer goods such as t-shirts, trainers, and plastic toys.

In her book *The China Price: the True Cost of Chinese Competitive Advantage*, Alexandra Horney asserts: *"The forces that will shape China's manufacturing sector in coming decades are already clear: rising wages and material costs, greater demand for unionization, a higher risk of litigation, a dwindling supply of cheap workers, calls for better product quality and safety, and substantial downward pressure on margins"* In 2007 it manufactured £1.1 trillion worth of products. By 2011, it was $2.9 trillion, surpassing the US at $2.43 trillion.

At the top end

Over the years as quality and competence of Chinese factories and workers improved, luxury goods such as Mercedes and BMW are being manufactured in China, along with high-ticket electronic goods. Indeed, VAG entered China in 1978 and is now one of the top car makers in China and exports to other Asia-Pacific markets. Late in 2012, Jaguar Land Rover agreed a joint venture with major Chinese manufacturer Chery to build cars in China, the first outside of the UK.

Consequently, China is amongst world's top consumer of cement and steel. Another example is that of chemical plants: in 2005 50 new plants worth over $ 1bn were installed. And that has not slowed much in the years since.

There is also local enterprise. Take for example *Zhong Guancun*. *Thirty* years ago it was a quiet suburb of Beijing with mostly green fields and some universities. Twenty years ago, small computer companies appeared outside the universities probably run by ex-students. Ten years later it grew into largest and most vigorous IT Park in China. 77% of companies set up here die in 3 years and many of rest die in another two, but nothing can stop more from starting and trying to grow.

In 1984, *Liu Chuanzhi* started a small company there called *Legend*, with only $25,000 and 11 employers. Today, after taking over IBM's PC division in 2005, it has grown into 25,000 employers and turnover of $15bn. Its name was changed to *Lenovo.* It has over 35% of China's PC market and 7% of the world market in 2009. In October, 2012 it grew to become the world's largest PC maker.

Although not in the same league as Boeing or Airbus, the Commercial Aircraft Corporation of China (Comac) has started to deliver 60 to 100 passenger jets competing with Bombardier and Embraer. These aircraft will be the workhorses as most of the new airports in China will not be in large cities and hence will not be designed to take super jumbos.

At the other end

At the other end of manufacturing is the story of _Yiwu_. It was a small town in _Zhejiang_ one of the most densely populated provinces, which includes Shanghai. It was early adopter of market economy and from 1982 it gradually turned itself into a huge manufacturing and marketing centre of consumer goods, from needles to pencils to Christmas kitsch. There are very few things you can't find here. Those you can't find and want will be made for you. With over 80,000 vendors stocking 3 million varieties in 1,700 categories of commodities made and sold here, things here are incredibly inexpensive. The Yiwu _Index_ is now one of the main deciding factors on the world price for the small commodities. Even so Yiwu made $10 billion sales in 2011.

So, the majority of the goods made in China are relatively low-priced consumer goods such as t-shirts, trainers, toys and consumer electronics. One of the world's largest container ships, Emma Maersk used to ply the route from China to Europe, can haul 11,000 containers filled with these goods. According to one source, in 2006 it carried from China: glasses, sports gear, shower gel and shampoo, clothes, furniture, carpets, laptop computers, make-up, toys, Christmas decoration, mobile phones, shoes, trainers games and puzzles, and TV sets. And it took back from the UK: plastic scrap, waste paper and card, waste electronic equipment, scrap metal and repairable electrical goods. But as one senior Chinese politician said: _"We need to export many container ships of toys and trainers to afford a single Boeing aircraft (B747-400 costs $250m before bulk discounts)!"_

In the middle

In between, China is no 1, 2 or 3 in most categories apart from aerospace and high-tech. For example it is no 1 in pianos, guitars and even 'panama' hats - though purists would say, *real* panama hats need to be made from an Ecuadorian reed. The name, incidentally, arose because engineers building the Panama Canal found these hats excellent for the equatorial climate. Of course many of the pianos and guitars are made under famous labels: such as Steinway and Yamaha - a consequence of contract manufacturing due to the China price.

Even in the matter of western suits, one firm, Trands, makes 5 million suits pa for labels such as Gap, Banana Republic and Marks & Spencer. But as in other sectors, more and more competition is coming from Vietnam, Philippines and Bangladesh, along with east European countries. Of course, Dalian Dayang Group, the world's largest suitmaker and maker of Trands suits, got a boost when Warren Buffett replaced his wardrobe by Trands suits and - it is said - so did his friend Bill Gates.

Service industries

According to the CIO World Factbook; the service industry in 2012 accounted for 44% of GDP (<33% of employment) while manufacturing accounted for 46% (>30% of employment), with agriculture at 10% (37% of employment). The target is for services to reach 50% of GDP by 2020. Hong Kong is seen as the model with services accounting for 90% of its GDP.

After the 2008-09 recession

China took the opportunity of the 2008-09 recession to reduce low end: 1,000 of 5,000 cheap shoe factories closed in 12 months; 500 out of 600 cigarette lighter factories closed in 18 months; and so on sector after sector.

It is amazing that that with 2m <u>migrant workers</u> laid off (out of 150m migrant workers) in 2008; with 40% of GDP attributed to export, China not only survived the recent recession, but it grew by 8.7% in 2009. This is because it stimulated the economy with nearly $600bn over two years - including increases in infrastructure spend, plus subsidies to replace old cars at 10 x the level of UK support. It also encouraged retail/consumer spending as well as encouraged bank lending.

The India-China bilateral trade was $74bn in 2011. But, China's export is 8 times that of India. In 2009 it overtook Germany to become world's number 1 exporter. And by 2012, it overtook America as the world's number 1 manufacturer.

4.8 India is not only the home of call centres, and business process outsourcing (BPO)

India's <u>services sector</u> contributed in 2011 to 57% of GDP (23% of employment), industry to 28% (14% employment); and agriculture to 16% (52% of employment). Although 70% of outsourcing is done for US or UK firms, the rest of the world is catching up. Consequently, language schools have sprung up in call cities with major call centre business teaching Spanish to cater for Latin American business, and many other languages. Since 2007, off-shored tutoring has been on offer. One of these is working with HarperCollins. Pearson has a similar service. Not only IT and BPO (business process outsourcing) is at play but also lawyers and architects. The latter is aided by the increasing use of computer aided design which is easier to do remotely.

Often, Indian firms set up offices in other countries to cater for neighboring clients, such as Wipro's Chengdu office in China caters for both Chinese and Japanese business and its Romanian office looks after French and Italian clients. The other reason is that there is both a shortage of suitable talent and increasing pay for those that do fit. Since 2011 there is anecdotal evidence that some US and UK firms are reversing the trend and moving some call centers back. This is mainly due to issues with customer service arising out of the lack of local knowledge by Indian operatives. But some think that the cost balance is shifting out of favor for outsourcers.

What has not been evident is that outsourcing is not only used by foreign firms but by Indian firms themselves, such as Birtel Telecoms. As in many countries Indian labor laws favor the employee. This has caused an issue with companies that wish not to have too many permanent staff and all the labor issues that pertain. Naturally, according to the Indian Labour Bureau, contract workers as a percentage of all workers have risen from under 16% to over 24% between 2000 and 2007. Another unique feature of Indian business is that whilst 4% of China's businesses employ less than 10 staff, India has a massive 89%. But problems are brewing as contract workers are typically paid less and have fewer benefits. But changes in labor laws will be slow in coming, as with many aspects of Indian 'bureaucracy'.

But India also has IT centers of excellence, pharma, auto, etc. Some 400,000 engineers graduate each year.

Indian major acquisitions include:

- Steel: India's Mittal Steel bought Acelor in France and Tata Steel bought Corus in Britain
- Cars: India's Tata Motors bought Jaguar-Land Rover and is making a great turnaround having weathered the recent recession. Tata, of course, is an old-fashioned conglomerate with 85 companies of which 27 are listed. It is into all sorts of other businesses including tea, power, telecoms and IT consulting and outsourcing.
- Inward Foreign Direct Investment FDI is increasing, companies like the UK insurer Prudential has sets its sights on Asia and forging alliances, such as with AIA based in Hong Kong but which covers India. Although China is big on personal savings, apparently India is even bigger, estimated at 30%. This augers well for financial services which need funds rather than those who wish to lend to consumers.
- Outward Foreign Direct Investment FDI now equal to inward FDI, but growing faster

During 2010-11:

- India's manufacturing overtook agriculture for the first time. It contributes above 20% to the economy, with agriculture around 20%, but employing nearly 60% of the population.
- Tata launched the Nano for the average Indian family and is producing 500 per day at their Ahmedabad plant, which is planned to double in 2012; ready for export in 2013.
- Inward investment doubled to $24bn
- $billionaires also doubled to 48
- 300 Special Enterprise Zones SEZs being set up
- 40% of top 340 multinationals plan to manufacture in India by 2012. In July 2011, two states are in contention to attract Peugeot-Citroen to build a $1bn car factory in Sanand, Gujarat to start operations in 2014. It will be the last of the major car firms to manufacture in India. According to OICA and International Organization of Motor Vehicle Manufacturers, India produced over 2.8m passenger vehicles in 2010 versus USA's 2.7m (China produced over 13m).
- Germany has become a major exporter of machine tools to India of £30bn in 2011 rising to £95bn by end of 2015.

- Additionally, the government has awaken up to the <u>importance of infrastructure</u> and is planning to spend over $500bn in the current five-year plan having only spent $200bn in the previous one.

Couple of examples

Pharma

The *Indian pharmaceutical Industry* is in front rank of India's science-based industries with capabilities in complex field of drug manufacture and technology. A highly organized sector, the Indian Pharma Industry is estimated to be worth $ 4.5bn, growing at about 8 to 9 % annually, 2010 projection $25bn. It boasts of quality producers and many units approved by regulatory authorities in USA and UK.

The sector is highly fragmented with more than 20,000 registered units. The leading 250 pharmaceutical companies control 70% of the market with market leader holding nearly 7% of the market share. It meets around 70% of India's demand for bulk drugs, drug intermediates, pharmaceutical formulations, chemicals, tablets, capsules, orals and injectibles and is an exporter, mainly to third world countries.

Following the de-licensing of the industry, industrial licensing for most of the drugs and pharmaceutical products has been eliminated. Manufacturers are free to produce drugs approved by the Drug Control Authority. The Industry, with its rich scientific talents and research capabilities, supported by Intellectual Property Protection regime is well set to take on the world market. In October 2011, GSK said it had earmarked $2bn for appropriate acquisitions in India.

Information technology

CISCO: in *Sold on India,* Business Week Nov 25, 2005: The networking giant sees an edge there, even with most competitors resolutely set on growth in China'. Partly because of earlier major investment in China and partly because of concern of local firms 'copying' Cisco technology; e.g. law suit against Huawei was settled out of court.

India is home to many of the top <u>IT services firms</u>: Wipro, Infosys, Satyam and *TCS* – Tata Consulting Services employs 160,000 in India and has its largest employment outside of India in US with 14,000 staff. TCS has a plan to be amongst the top 3 IT companies in each of the BRIC countries. In 2008-09 IT and BPO accounted for $60bn of which $46bn were exports.

Wages are rising in India and despite steady flow of new graduates, Indian IT services firms are now opening operations in Mexico, Brazil, Poland, and even China – to tap into local markets. Part of the reason is that only 15% of the fresh graduates are deemed suitable. So Infosys and others have set up their own universities to train up to 50,000 people a year.

In fact _IBM India_ has grown steadily since is now largest entity outside of US, over 100,000 employees in 2012. No 4 after TCS (220,000 based in India), Infosys (150,000 mostly in India) and WIPRO (130,000 mostly in India).

The recent recession hardly affected India as it is not yet a major exporter and consumer spending rose as well at the cost of household savings. The IT sector, while affected, was not impacted as the 'hard industries' would have been. Local industries were hardly affected.

4.9   Consumerism expands in both China and India

This section is mainly about China. But if you remember the phrase _'India is China 15 years ago'_, then be assured sooner rather than later, India will also be a major consumer nation.

With a burgeoning middle class estimated to be around 800m (500m Chinese and 300m Indian) of whom c1 million are millionaires according to Merrill Lynch and Capgemini' _World Wealth Report_ in June 2011, Chindia's demand for consumer goods and services is increasing both in quantity and quality. Western manufacturers, marketers and advertisers are finding Chindia a dream come true. Some major retailers have set up shop with success after they come to terms with differences in culture, competitors and, sometimes, even offering what the local consumer really want.

One of the reasons China and India did not experience the 2008-09 recession was because of expansion in consumer spending. After years of cajoling, the governments seem to have persuaded the public (or at least the affluent part) to spend more and save less. Chinese households save on average 26% of income and Indian households over 30%. In 2009, Chinese savings dropped to half at 12%.

Increasing affluence comes into play

As 350m of the Chinese population has been lifted from dire poverty to relative affluence in one generation, the average Chinese is extremely optimistic, dynamic and patriotic (three attitudes that made America great) with an emphatic 'can do' spirit, determined to leave the next generation even better off than one's own. As many American visitors have commented, the *'Chinese dream'* is bigger than the American dream and they are more impatient to realize it. The Chinese consumer market was estimated at $1.7 trillion in 2009. Credit Suisse in China predicts it will rise to $16 trillion in 2020. By then China should have surpassed the US market. The downside of this increasing affluence is that whereas China used to be self-sufficient in many commodities including soya beans and corn. A problem for all as some of these are also sources of alternative fuels.

India's upward drive is caused more by its demographics than by urbanization and general increase in affluence, though these come into play as well. India has one of the youngest populations in the world with 50% under 25 and, like their Chinese counterparts, wants more, better and sooner. They are less interested in saving for tomorrow than their parents and more willing to take risks, and to spend. Nevertheless, savings here are well above western levels. In August 2011, the total private stockpile of gold in India is estimated to be 18,000 tonnes - more than twice the 8,100 tonnes held in Fort Knox by the Federal Reserve.

With the spread of Western culture including the commercialization of Valentine's Day and Mothering Sunday, the consumer is enticed to spend on these 'celebrations'. An unlikely commercial success is Karuturi Global, a horticultural company in Bangalore the world's biggest grower of roses; much of it exported, but with increasing domestic purchases for these imported Western celebrations. So successful has it been, that it is acquiring 370,000 hectares of land in Tanzania, 1% of the agricultural land and seeking to buy land in Senegal also.

In September 2010, India revised its 'basket of goods - after 15 years - in calculating the RPI to include satellite TV in place of the traditional sari. This is in addition to replacing the dhoti by microwave ovens and so forth.

Retail financial services

Generali, a major Italian insurance firm, is no 1 in life & pensions in China through alliance with China National Petro Corp; AIG (founded in Shanghai in 1919) was no 1 is now no 2, UK's Prudential has set up;

HSBC (originally the Hongkong and Shanghai Banking Corporation set up in Hong Kong in March 1865 and in Shanghai one month later) and RBS is there too. BTW in China there is an estimated $200bn in personal savings to be managed.

Retailing

By early 2013, IKEA has 12 stores in China, Wal-Mart, Home Depot and Best Buy all have stores in China. B&Q has 40 stores in China, having started in June 1999 – these provide complete fittings for new apartments of c$8,000 for two-bedroom flat - unlike relatively small ticket spending in the UK. This is because unlike the West, 70% of new Chinese residences are empty shells. B&Q was making 60% profit before the recession, 10 times that of the domestic division in the UK. The big difference is that in the UK we have the term DIY (do it yourself); in China it is really DIFM (do it for me).

Many grocers such as Tesco and Marks & Spencer are established too. Though the stock includes products not found in western outlets such as turtles, snakes and other 'exotica'. China is expected to be the world's largest grocery market by 2014.

India still has some restrictive practices. For example, the UK food retailer Tesco has for years been trying to get entry. It nearly achieved that in 2011, but at the last minute the approval was not granted. Consequently, only 5% of India's $400m retail market. But limited approval was again granted in 2012 – with huge protests by small retailers and opposition politicians. The rest is run by millions of family-owned small businesses. And the market is estimated to double by 2015.

Consumer goods

Jewelery: India is probably no 1 for gold and China is rapidly becoming no 1 for precious stones after the US, having recently overtaken Japan.

Cigarettes: Gallaher, the maker of Benson & Hedges and Silk Cut cigarettes, is about to start its long-awaited push into the tobacco market of China as its locally produced cigarettes go on sale there for the first time.

Food & drink: The first joint-venture company, NESTLÉ Shuangcheng

Ltd., was established (Heilongjiang Province) in 1987. Coca Cola and Pepsi adverts are ubiquitous; as is KFC.

Health & beauty: L'Oréal is BIG in China; they also bought local firm who distributes cosmetics through 250,000 outlets! It has invested in research & development centers in both China and India. Apparently women in both countries like to appear whiter than the way they were born, and what counts for white face powder in the West is just not white enough. Also, Chinese faces are wrinkle free for much longer than Caucasian faces, but once wrinkles appear they occur at a faster rate. It also had to set up training schools. The Cultural Revolution created a generation gap in the tradition of make-up and hair styling - giving it an ideal opportunity to educate and sell at the same time. Chinese urban women spend 10 -15% of their salary on cosmetics and skin care, which adds up to $10bn a year and rising. Being China, there are some 4,000 cosmetic firms (c15% foreign owned) vying for that business. L'Oréal makes c$400m pa and rising. In 2006/7, L'Oréal set up hairdressing training schools and salons <u>in India</u>.

Appliances: The first purchase of a newly employed urbanite after a cooker is probably a TV set, then perhaps an air-conditioner followed by a refrigerator (buying fresh food is still preferred to buying once a week, though habits are changing). Despite the speedy nature of Chinese cooking, microwave cookers are also on the increase. A sign that the Chinese consumer is also short of time. 130m units of household appliances were sold in 2010 for China to become lead market.

Cars: Chinese consumers are now making and buying more cars than American counterparts. 4 million cars clog the roads of Beijing, where 12,000 new drivers' licenses are issued each week. The road improvement budget is $160bn in 2012. And the car industry resembles that of America before the General Motors consolidation of over a century ago. Vehicle sales in 2010 were partly stimulated by a *'cash for clunkers'* scheme not unlike that in the UK, except the incentives were much higher and the scheme lasted much longer. Some 100 plus car manufacturers compete, including pure indigenous makes to joint ventures to top marques such as Mercedes and BMW. DaimlerChrysler invested €1b in China in 2004 building Mercedes S-Class, and BMW the 7-Series in ShenYang a couple of years later. They tend not to bother with lower models. In late 2012, Jaguar Land Rover announced a JV with Chery to manufacture cars in China, as well as to develop models specific to China.

Having become number 1, 2 or 3 for the top mass car brands such as Mercedes and BMW, China is now drawing in the top sports brands such as Porsche, Lamborghini, Maserati and Ferrari. They all aspire to make China their number 1 market in the next few years. A big difference between China and India (and possibly elsewhere) is that whereas globally 5% of Maserati owners are women, 30% in China are women. Admittedly, some of these may be gifts from men buyers to women who are registered as the owner, but Maserati believes that 90% of the women owners are entrepreneurs in their own right.

The sheer numbers in China makes the mind boggle. For instance 55% of private cars in 2011 have yet to have new tires. This will in 3 to 5 years pose a great opportunity to not only tire makers, but would have created a shortage of rubber. Fortunately, Thailand has foreseen the opportunity and planted 128,000 acres of new rubber trees. They should be ready in 2020 when the tires on the 200 million private cars need replacing.

Luxury goods: apart from luxury cars, other luxury goods are in demand in a society well practiced in conspicuous consumption. Vertu mobile phones, diamond encrusted costing up to $100,000 fly off the shelves. There are apparently some people willing to pay $150,000 for a Hermès Birkin handbag at a Louis Vuitton shop – twice the price on eBay. The point of the exercise is, of course, to be seen to be able to afford such a bag.

Advertising: Martin Sorrell (chairman, WPP) says advertising in China set to out-grow Japan and then US in next few years.

Tourism: Both Chinese and Indians of means are used to touring their own country. Any foreign visitor will vouch for this. Increasingly, both Chinese and Indians are travelling abroad, to the delight of tourist boards at favored destination. In recent years, Indian tourists came to the UK in larger numbers than American tourists and spent more. Chinese tourists are predicted to overtake the Indians in the UK.

Both Chinese and Indian middle class consumers are becoming global tourists. Britain, in particular London, has hired Mandarin speakers in its high end stores. Some are starting to accept China UnionPay credit cards. In 2011, an estimated £500m was spent by Chinese tourists in British stores during the summer sales, never mind hotels, restaurants, theatres and tourist attractions. A similar amount was estimated for the Christmas and New Year sales. There is an estimated increase of between 10 and 15% in 2012.

4.10 Information Technology

There are significant differences between China and India as producers and as users of IT.

As producers or providers of technology

China is mainly known for hardware, but is gradually moving into software - still at US$5bn export compared to India's US$55bn export, though the total revenue of US$90bn is comparable to India's. In fact several Indian IT services companies including Tata Consulting Services have opened up <u>operations in China</u>, both to tap the talent as well as the market. Despite the large number of fresh engineering, science and maths graduates coming out each year, not all are of the requisite standard. For example, Infosys has opened up its <u>own 'university'</u> to ensure new recruits are of the right standard. Interestingly, the campus is host to not only Indian recruits but also foreigners from as far away as America and China.

Another exercise sponsored by Infosys is taking c90 low-caste and 'untouchable' students in Bangalore and training them in around six months to attain standards normally only achieved by the famous IIT graduates. Many of these graduates of this programme end up being employed by Infosys as well as its rivals Wipro, IBM and HP.

India is mainly known for software & services cUS$90bn pa, but <u>moving into hardware</u>. This is both in terms of indigenous companies and overseas firms. Many of the latter sense that putting their entire 'eggs in one Chinese' basket may not be strategically sound. India has 12 mobile providers to China's 3. India held an auction of 3G bandwidth in 2010 which raised $15bn that is reminiscent of Britain's in 2000.

Both have other technology industries; pharma, biotech …

Both turn out huge number of science and engineering graduates; though the numbers need to be taken with a bit of caution, particularly in India where some degrees are less equal than others!

Both are following a technology growth path proven by Japan in 60s & 70s and South Korea in 80s & 90s:

1. Cheap adequate 'copies' of foreign products, usually under license.
2. Low-cost good-quality substitutes, sometimes <u>bordering on copyright infringement</u>.
3. High-quality originals through indigenous innovation - eg <u>SunTech Power</u>, one of top 3 solar voltaic cell firms

As users of technology

China has more users of PCs and the Internet, especially amongst the urban middle class and students. It is targeted by companies like Apple who plan to expand from 7 (Dec 2012) to many more stores within next few years. So far there are no Apple stores in India. Obviously both China and India have numerous Apple retail resellers.

India has been slower in exploiting IT due to a larger rural poor population who have limited telecoms access; and also joint families which sometimes mean one PC or port per household. But the government has many ambitious plans to make great strides. In March 2010, India embarked on a scheme to provide its 630,000 villages with broadband internet access. The plan is to use the internet to provide education and health services and to bridge the gap between regions and castes. 2012 is the deadline to reach every village with a population above 300. When completed, 300 rural citizens will have access via their villages. The scheme is funded by the state-run Universal Service Obligation fund (worth about $3.5billion) into which private telecoms operators have to pay 5% of gross earnings.

Even without the new schemes, Indian farmers sell their produce through a shared intranet service provided by <u>ITC, major agri-business firm</u> ($3bn), cutting out the middle-man. The service also provides services to the farmers such as weather forecasts, advice on fertilisers and pesticides and so forth. Bureaucracy is slowly being beaten by publicly accessible Internet offices (<u>telecentres</u>) run by graduates for free, with all government forms are posted on the Internet. When fully operational, it will replace a bureaucracy established by the East India Company and refined by the Indian 'babu' (clerk) over 200 years.

Mobile phones are used by an increasing number of Indians both rich and poor. India's 850 million subscribers (mid-2011) are second only to China's of around 1 billion. Street letter-writers are being replaced by mobile phones where illiterate city migrant workers can talk to their rural relatives directly rather than by dictating letters. Reuters has a service <u>Reuters Market Lite</u> for farmers in several Indian states via SMS to mobile phones. For poorer villagers who do not own mobile phones, each village will have several for single-call rental at a reasonable price. Nearly 60% of Indian Internet users access the web via their mobiles and not PCs. NOTE: there are similar mobile applications in China, but PC access is much higher.

The figures below of uses of IT in 2012 come from different sources:

	China	India
PC	150m	50m
Broadband	380m	15m
Internet	560m	150m
Mobile	1.1bn	920m

India has invented a *'spoken web'* that exploits the higher penetration of mobiles versus the PC: Voicesites and VoiGen - http://tinyurl.com/c8o2lh9 .One of the great advantages of a spoken web to that of a 'written' one is that even illiterate farmers and city workers can articulate and hence communicate with each other or people who are literate. This is a major advantage in India where literacy is still a major issue.

The future of telecoms in India and China is mobile. China Mobile, China Unicom and Bharti Airtel are the top 3 mobile service providers in the world and are all still growing. Bharti Airtel is unique in that apart from sales and marketing, everything else is outsourced – taking India's own medicine. Its network (base stations, microwave links, etc.) is maintained by <u>Ericsson</u> and <u>Nokia Siemens Network</u>, business support by <u>IBM</u> and transmission towers by another company. Ericsson agreed for the first time, to be paid by the minute for installation and maintenance of their equipment rather than being paid up front. This enables the company to provide pan-India phone call rates of Rs. 1/minute (US$0.02/minute).

5 POLITICS: CHINA POST LIBERATION AND INDIA POST INDEPENDENCE

After economics, politics is the next key factor in understanding where China and India are and where they are likely to go.

In this chapter:

o   We start with a summary of the political situation in 2011-12 in China; followed by that of India.

o   We then compare India's democracy with China's autocracy, including federal versus centralist rule; followed by a military and colonial ambitions comparison, and closing with a comment on China's unique leadership for the past two decades.

o   Two pairs of pages that follow will cover:

    o   Chinese and Indian tensions

    o   Chinese and Indian geopolitics.

5.1   Recent Chinese politics

2013

In March 2013, Xi Jinping was confirmed as the new President and Li Keqiang as the new Premier. Both were near certainties for several years. They are likely to make some dramatic changes in Chinese politics.

Xi is seen to be 'of the people'. During the Cultural Revolution he was sent down to the farms as were many other urban youngsters at that time. But apparently he took to his new role with great enthusiasm and energy and is well remembered by the villagers. Soon after being affirmed as the new Party chief in November 2012 he toured several poor villages in a remote province to see for himself the great contrast between affluent urban living and poor rural life. Although he is an engineer by training and early experience, he is alone now amongst the seven-strong Standing Committee of the Politburo; whereas the previous two decades saw the majority of the then nine-member top leadership as engineers. Whether by design or accident, this augers well for China. It has spent the last 20+ years building infrastructure and manufacturing. It is time to consolidate and pay its attention to other more important issues – more later in this section. He is known to be forthright and relatively open. In his forthcoming visit to Africa, it is rumoured he will be bringing his wife - Peng Liyuan. Madame Peng is a popular 'pop star' in China and holds the rank of Major General in the People's Liberation Army. This will be a first for Chinese leaders since the 1940s when Madame Chiang – wife of KMT leader Chiang Kaishek - used to be treated as China's unofficial ambassador to the West esp to America. Their only child, a daughter, Xi Mingze, 20, attending Harvard University in Cambridge, Massachusetts, under a pseudonym. Xi himself has visited many foreign countries including the US.

Li is thought to be the most learned leader for generations. He has a PhD in law and is fluent in English, another first amongst Chinese leaders since the mid 20th century. Not only that, he is not shy to display is fluency by giving a major speech in Hong Kong in English in August 2011, thereby informally saying that it is ok for Chinese leaders to speak in a foreign language in public rather than to pretend to use interpreters. It is thought he is reform minded and the team of ministers and vice premiers he has assembled seem to reflect that. Many of the industry and economic chiefs are known to be interested in reducing more drastically the plethora of State Owned Enterprises (SOEs) which many economist believe hold back private enterprise.

Critical issues facing the new leadership of 2013-2022 as acknowledged by Xi and Li are:
- Rampant and pervasive corruption at all levels of government.
- Extravagant and conspicuous expenditure by officials both when on official business but also when on private affairs, such as lavish banquets at every opportunity and use of official cars for domestic purposes.
- Life-threatening pollution of water and air.

- Destabilising disparity between urban affluence and rural poverty – including the issue of c200 million migrant workers with limited rights in the cities where they toil ten months of the year.
- Excruciatingly slow move from an investment-led (manufacturing, building, mining, infrastructure and export) economy to a consumer-led one.
- Implicit property 'bubble' with large numbers of vacant properties built and bought for investment rather than for living in.
- Unsustainable debt held by provincial and district authorities, often used to finance these vacant properties or sometimes for ill-thought through factories.

In the context of these issues, all of which are internal, the territorial disputes with all its maritime neighbours pale into insignificance, as also China's seeming inability to rein in North Korea. And the on-going Tibetan dissidence and the latent Uighur unrest in Xinjiang are also secondary compared to the issues listed above.

As President Xi has said, unless these issues are resolved within the next decade, there is no assurance that the people will continue to accept single-party Communist rule as a given.

2012, of course, was dominated by the _decennial change in national leadership_. This time round, seven of the nine members of the Central Politburo Standing Committee of the Communist Party of China (CPC) retired in November at the 18th National Congress of the CPC due to the mandatory age limit of 68. At the same time the number was reduced to seven to make consensus decision-making easier.

The two who continued, Xi Jinping and Li Keqiang respectively became President and Premier, when the incumbent President Hu and Premier Wen retired in March 2013.

2012 was also marked by a *major political scandal* involving Bo Xilai and his wife Gu Kailai. He was until the scandal which broke in mid-year a very charismatic leader who governed a major province in North East China and successfully grew Chongqing into the fourth unitary metropolis (after Beijing, Shanghai and Tianjin). He was deemed to be a bit of a 'revisionist' harking back to the 'good old days' under Chairman Mao. Unfortunately for him and his wife, the scandal first involved the police chief of Chongqing trying to defect at the American embassy. It turned out that he was reporting the alleged murder of a British businessman and family friend of Bo and Gu. That then unravelled, with Gu arrested and subsequently tried and found guilty of murder, Bo, in the meantime, was ejected from the party for misconduct and possible corruption. As of late January 2013, his trial has yet to take place.

2012 was also a year of many public protests and many *reforms*. To name a few of the reforms:

o   More sympathetic <u>petition handling</u>
o   Better <u>public health</u>
o   Improved <u>mental health</u>
o   Increased <u>retirement</u> pension
o   Improved <u>food safety</u>
o   Tighter <u>judicial reform</u>
o   Curb to <u>police abuse</u>
o   Control over <u>over-spending by officials</u>
o   Improved <u>migrant workers' rights</u>
o   And many more.

The biggest spur to reforms is the increasingly voice of the people – not only through public protest, which is on the increase – but also via social media. Sina Weibo, a cross between Twitter and Facebook, carries more public protest and dissent than all the other social media in the West put together. Government has realized it cannot stop this as the internet is now part of the fabric of life for the growing middle class in China. So the only recourse is to make reforms when it can.

The one area where reform is not being mentioned is in politics and *democracy*. That may be a reform too far. However, the five new members of the Central Politburo Standing Committee will all be retiring in 2018. They are uniformly not deemed to be reformists by nature. So perhaps when Xi and Li pick their own team of five in 2018 we may yet see political reform. That will also depend crucially on how the economy will have done.

China is no longer expecting double digit growth, but a 7 to 8% growth is still needed to ensure enough new jobs are available for the growing population; however small that growth is due to the continuing one-child policy, though even that is being debated.

Until 2012, there had been a simmering tension around *disputed territory* in South China Sea with China's claims to a whole host of small islands, mostly uninhabited through its declaration of a wide sea boundary. In 2102, this tension erupted into several incidents involving most of the neighboring countries including Japan, the Philippines, Vietnam and Indonesia.

Unfortunately Japan exacerbated the tension by nationalizing disputed islands. This caused a public outcry in China resulting in Japanese cars and car showrooms being torched. So much so that Toyota, Nissan and Honda all showed depressed figures in September and October.

China then went on the offensive and in mid-November added a map to its passport showing disputed territories as within its boundary. That also included Himalayan areas disputes with India. Consequently, the countries who are in disagreement including Vietnam, Taiwan and India, are countering by taking steps such as stamping visas on attached paper rather than in the Chinese passports.

Despite assurances from both China and India that the border issue is not critical, India has been beefing up its Himalayan defenses and sending its navy to South China Sea to protect its oil and gas interests there.

In late November, Hainan Province, charged with overseeing the South China Sea issue, unilaterally declared that its armed patrol boats have the right to board foreign ships in the disputed waters. This has, naturally, sent up the temperature several degrees.

Mr Obama is pouring oil on trouble waters by announcing a collaboration pact around the Pacific that excludes China. And the November summit of ASEAN nations exhibited dissent for the first time, with China almost in total isolation.

The territorial disputes, if not, resolved soon, could be the source of major disruption as all the neighbors are strong trading partners with China and the disputed waters is a major shipping channel for a major part of goods from and to China, yet where national sovereignty is concerned, nations often become irrational. Unfortunately, towards the end of 2012, Japan re-elected its right wing party and their attitude is much tougher than the outgoing party's. Wars have been fought about disputed territories in the past and who is to say it will not happen in the Pacific region again. God forbid.

2011

Although China has leapt forward in so many endeavours, the major high-speed train crash in Wenzhou in July 2011 exposed it to concerns about *safety and corruption* issues. This incident caused a major pause in the ambitious railway building programme which was resumed in the middle of 2012.

Then there is the widely publicised confrontation between ordinary villagers at a relatively small village of 20,000 citizens, Wukan and the local authorities concerning illegal and corrupt land seizures that eventually got central government involved in a compromise - something not often heard of in China. As there are estimated to be 100,000s of *public protests and mass demonstrations* of this kind, this incident may, perhaps, mark a watershed in how the central government deals with the more serious of these issues.

5.2   Recent Indian politics

2013 saw the long expected inclusion of Rahul Gandhi into the ruling circle of the National Congress Party. His reluctance may be partly due to the fact that both his father, Rajiv and his grandmother Indira were assassinated. But it could also be due to his natural inclination not lead with a high-profile front.

The Congress party met with major losses in important state elections in 2012. It needs to declare national general elections before May 2014 but that is likely to take place earlier than that. Prime Minister Singh is due to retire and there is no obvious successor. So Congress is gearing itself, with the reluctant leadership of Rahul. If state elections are any indicator, majority re-election is far from assured for Congress. Time will tell whether he proves to be an asset or not in the 2014 national elections.

Communal/sectarian strife, both Hindu-Muslim and anti-Christian, continues as also the Naxalite insurgency. Fortunately, nothing untoward happened between India and Pakistan. And until late November, there was no visible tension between India and China. But, as the previous section indicated, due to the printing of a map in new Chinese passports that show disputed areas as belonging to China, a new row has flared up.

Sadly a major anti-*corruption* bill was passed by the Lokh Sabha (lower house) but rejected by the Rajya Sabha (upper house). But it is not dead as the activists formed a <u>new party</u> in 2012.

Despite this set back, India has taken some draconian actions to signal its fight against corruption. In July, it banned the sale of huge stockpiles of iron ore that were mined by illegal entities. These operations going on since 1990s when mining was liberalized. Chief Minister of Karnataka was arrested along with several industrialists. India is no 3 in iron ore. The consequent drop of 23% in exports caused the market to shoot up sharply. In September, India decided to auction off the illegally mined ore, keeping 10% as compensation for lost tax revenues.

2012 saw the gradual easing of restraints to *foreign investment* in the retail field. Though public protests by small retailers have erupted from time to time, sometimes causing government to add restrictions such as to IKEA.

5.3 Democracy versus autocracy

India is the world's largest democracy. But it feels more like a hereditary dynasty with continuity from Nehru, to Indira Gandhi, to Rajiv Gandhi and now Sonia Gandhi (who calls the shots behind the scenes) of the National Congress Party – which won conclusively in the last national elections; with her son Rahul waiting in the wings. The National Congress Party ruled from 1947 to today: (except 1977-80 and 1998–2004). In many ways India is a single-party democracy.

Democracy seems to work in India. But economic and industrial progress, especially in the area of state-funded and led infrastructure is moving at a much slower pace than China.

China is the world's largest so-called Communist state. But it is more market-oriented and capitalist than many Western nations - some of which are more socialist. In reality there are only c80m registered party members (around 6% of the population); in same order of magnitude as registered Christians of c60m. One estimate says that there are as many Communist millionaires as non-Communist in China. The Chinese

Communist Party has ruled since 1949, a 'centralised' single-party autocracy.

Although transition from one President to the next has not always been smooth, China has avoided the violent transitions of the Russian leadership. President Hu retired from his party leadership post in 2012 and Vice President Xi Jingping_ succeeded him. BTW - Xi is another Chinese leader with an engineering degree (Chemical Eng from Tsinghua University).

Xi's also took over from Hu as chairman of the party's Central Military Commission (CMC) makes him the second civilian member of the CMC, after Hu, who serves as chairman. According to the party's practice, only the CMC chairman and his potential successor can be civilian members of the supreme command of the country's armed forces, all other members being career military officers. The CMC chairmanship is a post that the general secretary of the party takes to uphold the principle of *'the party commands the gun'*.

Xi ascended as the state President at the National People's Congress (NPC), China's parliament, in March 2013.

A view is developing that autocratic *'state capitalism'* such as in China, Russia, Singapore and the Gulf States really work, at least in terms of economic gain.

Federal versus centralist rule

India practices a federal structure where states have a high degree of autonomy. For example <u>West Bengal</u> and <u>Kerala</u> have enjoyed Communist rule for decades until a couple of years ago. However, a <u>state of emergency</u> was declared three times:

1. Between October 26, 1962 to January 10, 1968 during the <u>India-China</u> war — *'the security of India'* having been declared *'threatened by external aggression'*.
2. Between December 3, 1971 to 1977 originally proclaimed during the <u>Indo Pakistan war,</u> and later extended along with the third proclamation — "the security of India" having been declared "threatened by external aggression".
3. Between June 26, 1975 to March 21, 1977 under controversial circumstances of political instability under the <u>Indira Gandhi</u>'s <u>Prime Ministership</u> — "the security of India" having been declared "threatened by internal disturbances".

Some analysts attributed the Sikh separatist movement to have been accelerated by the third state of emergency. That, of course, led in 1984 to the assault on the <u>Golden Temple</u> at Amritsar and in turn tragically led to the <u>assassination of Indira Gandhi</u> by her two Sikh bodyguards.

China practices a more centralist structure. However, due to the vast size of the country and the populous provinces, not all central laws or edicts are enforced with equal vigour by local authorities. On our web page covering <u>'green' issues</u> we showed how local economic interests sometimes subvert central attempts to curb pollution. In addition, over the years, with four <u>direct-controlled municipalities</u> of Beijing, Shanghai, Tianjin and since 1997 Chongqing - accounting for some 80m population, plus the plethora of <u>Special Economic Zones</u>, together with the <u>Special Administrative Regions</u> of Hong Kong and Macao; central government's sway on local matters is not always as clear as Beijing would like. But for a country of 1.3bn, centralism is still very evident.

Military comparison

The <u>military structure</u> in **India** of over 1m personnel is loosely based on the British India Army, with a <u>combination of regiments</u> that are geographic/ethnic-based and others more general. So there is a Sikh regiment, even after the problems arising out of Indira Gandhi's assassination, Assam, Madras and Gorkha's; and Guards, Grenadiers and several armoured regiments. Each regiment keeps traditions that started with the British, regimental flags with battle honours (mostly gained during the two World Wars on behalf of Great Britain). And dress uniforms that are really colorful.

    The <u>military structure</u> of **China** is geographic with each of seven military regions mapping onto several provinces. However, most of the regional commanders do not stay in one region too long and tend to rotate. This is a reaction to the time of regional warlords in the early half of the last century after the fall of the Ching (Manchu) dynasty and the stability of Chiang Kai-shek's KMT rule. There are over 2m active personnel and 1m active reserves. These figures exclude paramilitary forces of perhaps another 4m.

Colonial ambitions?

Although both countries have fought wars since their modern inception, these have mainly been border conflicts. In the case of India with Pakistan and with China. In the case of China, apart from its role in the Korean War (which it saw as supporting its neighbour and protecting its own integrity), with India, Russia and Vietnam.

Historically, neither country has had colonial ambitions. Nearly all the wars battles have been either against invaders, such as King Porus who fought Alexander to a stalemate or various princely states versus the East India Company; or the Chinese against 'barbarians' from the Steppes or against the Western powers a couple of centuries ago. The only 'aggression' that can be attributed to China is the annexation of Tibet and the Uighur territories (now Xinjiang, or new province) of western China. But the Chinese would see that as consolidation of tributary regions rather than invasion of foreign territory. Though Kublai Khan did attempt an invasion of Japan only to be thwarted by Kamikaze, the divine wind.

Despite the travels of Admiral Zheng He (1371 - 1433) who is purported to have sailed as far as east Africa, China did not create any colonies. The large populations of Indians in Africa are due to British imports of 'cheap labour', ironically turned on its head today with outsourcing. And the large populations of Chinese throughout SE Asia are what we would term today as 'economic migrants', with the San Francisco population due to import of cheap labour for the railways and gold mines.

Unique Chinese national leadership – until 2012

What is not commonly known is that for 20 years members of the Standing Committee of Politburo of Communist Party of China were engineers, not only by training by also by practice in their early careers. All 9 of the top leaders in the decade to 2002 and 8 of 9 top leaders in the decade to 2012. No wonder China's focus on infrastructure, manufacturing and technology.

By contrast, Western leaders seldom have a science or technology background with a few rare exceptions; Angela Merkel – physics being one and Mrs Thatcher - Chemistry, in the past, being another.

The other Western leaders have backgrounds in political science, law and economics.

When faced with problems the natural tendency of engineers is to find solutions, they strive to 'do better'; lawyers go for damage limitations, they 'prepare for the worst'. Politicians end up creating more laws. Of course, they say when you get three economists together you end up with six different theories.

However, with the new leadership of seven of 2012 include only two engineers. Perhaps China will take a more humanist view of developments and progress.

5.4 China's internal tensions are more significant than its external tensions

China's internal tensions

There are three main sources of tensions: ethnic, economic and social.

Ethnic tensions

These revolve round Tibetans and Uighurs. Tibetans mostly reside in Tibet to the south west and in some areas of Sichuan, Qinghai, Gansu and Yunnan provinces. The latter mostly in Xinjiang to the far west.

Various accusations such as cultural genocide, ethnic marginalisation through mass inward migration of the majority Han and religious repression have been made at the Chinese government. The reality is different. Several learned papers have not found support for these accusations. Nevertheless, there is great tension, periodically surfacing in the form of anti-Han riots.

The truth of the matter is that both Tibetans and Uighurs are being pushed into the 21st century from a pseudo-feudal, 'middle ages' culture. Many of the young Tibetans and Uighurs are torn between today's materialism and creature comforts and their traditional customs and norms. This is not to deny pro-Han policies, not least in language. But there is no overt religious suppression that some western media would like to portray. The Chinese government is hoping that as economic prosperity continues, and the older generation dies out, the tensions will reduce and perhaps even disappear.

In the case of Tibet, China is looking forward to the day when his holiness the <u>Dalai Lama will pass from this world</u> and they can appoint his successor. That is likely to be the trigger for another round of violence as the traditionalists will insist on searching for his re-incarnation in the accepted manner and will not accept any Beijing-supported successor.

<u>In the case of Uighurs</u>, China is wary of any link with Muslim extremism. They know they have to tread ever so cautiously. Any over-reaction is likely to push moderate Uighurs into the arms of the extremists.

Economic tension

This is an underlying phenomenon. It was the disparity between the rich capitalists and landowners, and the poor peasants and factory workers that enabled Mao and his fellow revolutionaries to establish a foothold and with the defeat of the Japanese, fight the KMT and takeover. The Chinese leadership is keenly aware that unless the majority of Chinese can enjoy a minimum level of living standard, unrest is not far below the surface. It was therefore with great relief that China found that millions of economic migrants who lost their factory-based urban jobs were able to move back to their rural hometowns without any major incidents. This avoidance was partly achieved through major injection into capital infrastructure projects that one analyst estimated at absorbing over half the displaced workers.

So they continuing policy is to help improve the economic conditions of the rural citizens. Fortunately, some of the great leap forward in urban economic levels has been distributed to rural communities through the thrift of the workers and the tradition of remitting as much as they can afford to the families back home, often by living frugally and foregoing luxuries of any sort. But <u>economic disparity</u> between rural and urban populations and between the affluent coastal regions and the interior continue and some believe is widening.

Some industries are still *sub-standard*. Mining is a prime example with <u>frequent accidents</u> that are rare in developed nations with health and safety laws. Many industrial plants are also sources of serious pollution. Despite <u>central government efforts</u> at curbing pollution at source, local authorities often connive with factory owners to avoid anti-pollution schemes in the cause of productivity or profit. At regular intervals when serious incidents occur, the public have <u>taken to the streets</u>.

Social tensions *and* **human rights** *issues*

These are on the rise in China. No longer is the citizen willing to accept the State's dictat without question. This new-found rebelliousness is helped along by the Internet and mobile phones. The authorities are finding it increasingly difficult to control the flow of information and the media is no longer the only way people find out what is happening. 'Slum' clearance - eviction issues, pollution problems, corruption by officials are all finding their way into the public domain, often triggering local incidents that increasingly get picked up by some of the national media.

What really makes the ordinary citizen mad is the *<u>corruption</u>* amongst officials that goes on at all levels. Despite regular purges and even <u>executions</u>, the rewards are so great that many an official will take the risk. Once again, the Internet is coming to the aid of the ordinary person in <u>exposing corruption</u> and not allowing local officials to sweep bad news under the carpet.

Human rights **and the** *rule of law* are still not to standards in most developed nations.

China is becoming aware that human rights is not something being stirred up by visiting western leaders but a real issue that it has to deal with. Ironically, the more affluent people become the more they become aware of their rights.

For example, Ai Weiwei, a renowned artist, who helped design the Bird's Nest Olympic stadium <u>and several other activists were detained in Chengdu</u> in August 2009 to prevent them attending the trial of a campaigner investigating schoolchildren's deaths in the Sichuan earthquake of 2008. The subject had become highly sensitive because of allegations that shoddy construction, linked to corruption, was <u>to blame for the high death toll in schools</u>.

Ai said a policeman punched him in the head in that incident, leaving him with painful headaches, and he underwent surgery in Germany weeks later after doctors spotted internal bleeding. He lodged a formal complaint

On August 10, 2010, Ai went to Chengdu's police department, to ask for a receipt of the complaint. But it refused and referred him to the police station at Jinniu. He said that as he arrived at the Jinnui police station he was surrounded by men who assaulted him and his assistant, and told him: *"If you want justice, go back to the US."* Ai lived in America for several years but is still a Chinese citizen.

In 2007 a famous *'nail house'* was demolished in Chongqing after months of stand-off when the owner refused to move until the authorities offered fair compensation. That repeated itself in 2012 with another high-profile house in the middle of a nearly finished highway to a new railway station.

Strikes, suicides and serious work- or environment-related *illnesses* are increasingly in the news. Workers at Honda went on strike. As one activist said: Workers are realising that their economic poverty is due to their political poverty. That is beginning to change. Additionally, China seems to be changing its 'no strike' laws. Guangdong province is planning to experiment in 2010 a law that would allow workers to strike. If this does not cause major incidents, observers believe it will be rolled out across the country over the next few years.

Suicides forced Foxconn a major electronics contract manufacturer (Apple, Dell, Sony, etc) to increase wages by over 70%. Foxconn may be an extreme example of the factory-city model. It employs over 1 million workers in China across 16 huge city-like campuses with sports facilities and entertainment centres. But these are hardly used as the workers are too exhausted after their long shifts. The suicides at Foxconn is being studied seriously as some psychologists see it as symptomatic of the way young, poor rural workers are drawn away from their hometowns to live in cheerless, soulless dormitories, with wages that in theory should be enough to sustain some form of social life, but in practice with as much spare cash as they can afford being remitted to families back home, there is hardly any social life at all.

Serious health problems at Wintek who supplies Apples iPhone due to use of n-hexane caused Apple to audit their Chinese suppliers. It found that 54% breached the 60-hour maximum weekly limit and 35% failed to meet wage and -or benefits requirements.

The net result is that in the medium term China will no longer be the low-cost manufacturing centre of the world. And either prices will rise (which will be a good thing as it will slow down rampant consumerism and the 'throw it away' culture) or manufacturing will move to low labour-cost economies elsewhere.

Public healthcare was in decline after the market reforms following the Cultural Revolution, when previously medical care was free either in the communes or through local administration. However, the government realised the situation and in 2008 launched '*Healthy China 2020*' to set up a universal health service across the country, available to even the poverty stricken, rural segment of the population, not unlike the British National Health Service.

In January 2012 a non-government organisation has been allowed to bring a court case concerning cancer caused by pollution from a factory. This is unprecedented and is the first sign of opening up of courts to private litigation.

There are two serious demographic concerns

Sociologists are concerned about:

Sex disparity

The single-child policy combined with the desire for a son, especially amongst the rural community means that within a decade China will have a shortage of 30 to 40 million women for men between the ages of 20 and 45. Officials are promulgating *'value your daughter'* slogans. But whether the rural poor will listen is another matter. They are also trying to curb the adoption of baby girls by foreigners. But nobody has any idea how that scale of disparity between the sexes will play out. Only time will tell. There is increasing pressure to change this policy soon.

Aging population

Unlike India, China's population will be aging and that China may well grow old before it has a chance to grow rich, at least on a per capita basis. By 2050, 1/3 of the population will be retirees! Storing up trouble for the next few decades.

In view of the two demographic 'time-bombs' China is slowly relaxing its one-child policy. For example, if at least one of the parents is a single child, the couple may be permitted more than one child. Similarly, in rural counties, if the child is a girl, a couple will be permitted a second child. However, many demographic experts believe these actions will not be in time to diffuse either of the time-bombs. Worse still, many of the young people interviewed have got used to the one-child policy and sees having more than one a significant burden and may not go for it even if permitted.

China's external tensions

Putting to one side geo-political issues such as the continuing pressure from the US to rebased the Renminbi (RMB) currency, global pressure regarding green issues, and the incessant search for more fuel and minerals to power the country and its industry, the main source of external tensions are China's relationship with its neighbours.

China has gone to war with the UN in Korea, with India, Russia, Burma and Vietnam

With India, Russia and Burma regarding disputed borders. That with Vietnam was purportedly due to a growing series of anti-Chinese issues; and presumed to be closed though there is on-going tension regarding the Paracel Islands, rich in oil and natural gas. The disputes with Russia have been settled. In fact, recent press would have it that Russia is negotiating with China to increase its investment in some of its major state-held energy companies by c$29bn. But that with India has still to be resolved. There are also on-going disputes with Japan over fishing rights and oil/gas rights.

Maritime disputes with its neighbours flared up in 2012

In the second half of 2012, disputes based on what neighbouring countries deem a unilateral and unreasonable East China and South China Seas territorial claim by China flared up. Even pressure at the AEAN conference in Cambodia did not move China. Unless these disputes are resolved soon, the tendency is for matters to accelerate and may well end up with multi-party military action. Especially as, at the end of 2012, Japan returned its right wing party back to power.

The other main source of tension is with *Taiwan*

On the one hand, not only is trade between the two very high and continues to expand, but many Taiwanese companies have opened both R&D and production centres in China, often dwarfing facilities in Taiwan itself. On the other hand, China believes that Taiwan is just another province and not an independent entity. As long as the Taiwanese government does not mention the i-word (independence) everything is hunky dory. But as soon as the i-word gets mentioned, China reacts violently and sometimes demonstrably so. Fortunately, Ma Ying-jeou, the incumbent won the 2012 Presidential elections in Taiwan. He is pro-Beijing and will reduce tensions brought about by Obama's declaration to strengthen its armed presence in the Pacific.

In the meantime, direct commercial flights were implemented in 2008, saving business people and tourists the long-winded journey via Hong Kong; also in 2008 a pair of 4-year old pandas were sent to Taiwan; and in June 2010 a significant trade accord (Economic Cooperation Framework Agreement) was signed that is equivalent to a free-trade agreement; and in September a culture agreement is being discussed by Cai Wu, the highest-ranking mainland official to visit the island in 12 years, with is Taiwanese counterpart. A most recent reconciliation move is the reunion of a Yuan Dynasty scroll that had been split in two in 1650: '*Dwelling in the Fuchun mountains*'. One short fragment lay in a mainland provincial museum, the other was taken across to Taiwan in 1949. They were reunited at the Taiwan National Museum in June 2011.

There is a solution that neither party wishes to entertain, that of a Special Administrative Region such as Hong Kong and Macau. China does not want to accept that, at least not at present; and to Taiwan, it will be a first step towards being 'swallowed' by China.

5.5   India suffers from both internal and external tensions.

For India the main sources are the yet-to-be eradicated caste system - outlawed since independence over 60 years ago - together with disparity between urban and rural population on the one hand and haves and have not's resulting in a continuing 'Maoist' insurgency, plus sub-surface antipathy between extreme Hindus and Christians and, of course, between Hindus and Muslims, exacerbated by the yet-to-be resolved Kashmir issue, leading onto Indo-Pakistan suspicions.

India's internal tensions

Similar to China, there are three main sources of tensions: economic, social and ethno-religious.

Economic tensions

Since 1967 there has been a growing spread of the Naxalite insurgency. The name derives from Naxalbari a village in West Bengal where peasants rose against the authorities. It is based on Maoism. And it has now spread across the so-called Red Corridor, holding sway over 40% of the geographic area. The government regards them as more threatening than the situation in Kashmir. Sometimes they are termed the 'red Taliban'. The Red Corridor, interestingly, connect the two Communist-ruled states of West Bengal to the north east and Kerala to the south west. Though both governments - until 2011 elections, run by the Communist Party of India (Marxist) - disclaim any link with the insurgents who are supported and sponsored by the break-away Communist Party of India (Maoist).

The Naxalites have been credited with several train derailments, the blowing up of rural police stations and attacks on other establishments. With the widespread nature of the insurgency, India cannot easily bring its armed forces to bear and has to rely on local police and paramilitary forces. Like guerrilla forces everywhere, when the authorities show up, the rebels melt into the background or, in some cases, the jungle.

The root cause for the continuing strength of the Naxalite movement is the ongoing disparity between the rich and poor, between the urban and rural 'economies'. Sadly, although there are grand plans, it is not clear how they will be implemented and what the consequences will be.

For example, big Indian cities have huge slums, none bigger than Dharavi (of *Slum Dog Millionaire* fame) in Bombay. It was going to be replaced by a modern metropolis as the land is estimated to be worth $10bn under the Mumbai Slum Rehabilitation Authority. But the plans of the MSRA do not show where and how the c600,000 residents (out of c6m slum dwellers in Bombay) were going to be re-housed! Also, there were no clear plans of what would happen to its industry that contributes c $1bn to the economy.

93

There is also serious tension between farmers and industries. In 2007 the <u>Nano micro car factory</u> planned by Tata in the outskirts of Calcutta had to be disbanded due to violent demonstrations by farmers. And in 2010, sugarcane farmers demanded a <u>sugar factory be handed over</u> to them. There have also been disputes over water, such as <u>over-exploitation by Coca Cola</u> factories. Although quite different on the surface, all three incidents (and there are many more) are about compensation, about fair land valuation and usage of scarce resources. Worse still, with uncertain monsoons and uncertain commodity prices, exacerbated by debt at often extortionate rates, <u>suicides amongst Indian farmers</u> is causing the authorities to examine the problems of rural life.

Last, but not least, of the economic tensions is the excruciatingly slow improvement to infrastructure, be it transport, water, power, etc. India needs to focus on these investments if it is ever to lift its poor as much as China has done. And part of the problem is the high and <u>pervasive corruption</u> that not only diverts investments but coupled with trenchant bureaucracy, hinders development. Matters have got to such a state that some larger private companies are developing local infrastructure to cater for its employees. For example, Mahindra and Infosys have joined forces to build a 1,500 acre city 50km south of Chennai to house up to 100,000 workers with a third living in a 325 acre residential zone. This city will be modern provided with utilities up to first-world standard, including power station, hospitals, roads, railway station, schools and sewage plant. The state government has been given 10% stake which has helped to secure licenses and other approvals. A second city near Jaipur that is twice a big has started.

Social tensions

In the <u>previous pages</u> we have covered India's continuing problems due to the ingrained caste system which although outlawed since independence over 60 years ago is still in place, particularly in rural areas. Three things are causing this to be a lessening problem:
1. Continuation of various public affirmative actions such as reserved places in higher education and government for lower caste and c180 million out-caste people (Dalits). This has led to some <u>castes wanting to be downgraded</u> as lower than traditionally structured to obtain access to better quotas; a 'race to the bottom' if you will.

2. Avoidance of caste differences in many large companies and in urban environment. This is partially good in that a lower caste or Dalit can work in, say, IT in Bangalore without any discrimination. But the moment he steps off a train or bus at his local town or village, he is back where his ancestors were thousands of years ago. For instance, he <u>cannot marry a woman in a higher caste</u> without endangering them both and possibly their families. In many rural areas, police turn a blind eye to murders over these love affairs or marriages. For Hindus, caste is timeless and irrevocable.

3. <u>Conversion at a steady rate to Buddhism by Dalits continues</u>. An estimated 10 million Buddhists practice in India, a steady increase. There is also some conversion to Christianity, but for many Christianity is 'foreign' whereas Buddhism is 'native'.

As we have mentioned before, Mayawati, the self-styled 'queen of Dalits' is fighting a <u>political battle for Dalits </u>as chief minister of Uttar Pradesh, one of India's most populous states and also one of the most prejudiced.

Nevertheless, Hindu extremists take this as an affront; and some <u>Hindu-based political parties</u> stir up caste issues to gain political advantage.

China is often accused of human rights infringements. In the opinion of this author, India's treatment (de facto if not de jure) of its Dalits and other tribal/aboriginal peoples is far worse.

Ethno-religious tensions

India continues to experience periodic sectarian violence: Hindu vs Muslim, Hindu vs Christian, and upper vs lower castes. Sometimes it takes a traffic accident involving several members of one religion to start a major riot as <u>happened in 2007 in Agra,</u> city of Taj Mahal after 4 Muslims were killed by a lorry. At other times a murder of a prominent person of one religion purportedly by someone from another can trigger major riots as happened in 2008 when <u>60 churches were burnt </u>after the murder of the Hindu leader Swami Lakshmananda Saraswati, along with four other activists from the hard-line Vishwa Hindu Parishad (VHP) party. The VHP originally claimed Christians were to blame for the deaths, but Maoist guerrillas have since claimed responsibility.

If marriage between people of different castes causes violence in villages, then <u>inter-religion marriages</u> can cause whole villages to be burnt to the ground.

After independence in 1947 and since 1950, some 18 <u>new states</u> have been established; mainly due to untenable tensions between different ethnic groups in the older larger states.

Political tensions

As India becomes more affluent, it is also becoming more dissatisfied with how things work, especially in the political arena. The growing middle class, mostly urban, feels it is marginalized by the rural poor who seem to carry the most votes. As one commentator said: *"the state is not about what it can do for me; but rather what can I do in spite of the state"*. The middle class regards politician with contempt, and government is seen as an obstacle for getting things done. The imbalance is that for politician, the cities are sources of income while the villages are the sources of power. This situation will not last for long. Sooner rather than later, the middle class will revolt.

India's external tensions

As detailed in <u>other pages</u>, there have been several *Indo-Pakistani* Wars:
- **1947**: Pakistan occupies one third of Kashmir (which India claims as its territory).
- **1965**: India attacks Pakistan on all fronts after attempts by Pakistani troops to infiltrate into Indian controlled Kashmir.
- **1971**: India decisively defeats Pakistan resulting in the independence of Bangladesh
- **1999**: Kashmiri insurgents backed by Pakistani troops capture Indian army posts. Indian Army retaliates and recaptures the posts.

As we said on the preceding page the border dispute with *China*, which resulted in a war in 1962, has not been resolved.

There was also a period of tension with *Sri Lanka* when the Indian army supported the Tamil Tigers. But with the defeat and practical annihilation of the Tigers, this tension has been diffused.

In summary, despite the short-looking list of external tensions, India's external tension with Pakistan especially over Kashmir, is on a par with its internal tensions.

5.6 *China* is adept at geopolitics; *India* is playing catch-up

Geopolitics is the application of the influence of political and economic geography on the politics, national power, foreign policy, etc, of a state. Politics as they affect the whole world.

However, China's game needs to be viewed in the light of a 2009 statement by the then leader-in-waiting VP Xi Jinping: *"First, China does not export revolution. Second, China doesn't export hunger and poverty. Third, China doesn't come and cause you headaches. So what's more to be said?"*

Xi's first point refers to Russia's and Cuba's past approach. His second refers to past colonialism. And his third to the West's insistence that economic and military aid comes with strings. Strings of democracy, human rights and so forth. And berates many for lack of transparency or human rights.

More interesting is what Martin Ivens, London's Sunday Times political correspondent wrote in Jan 2011: *"Twenty years ago, after the Tiananmen Square 'incident, ... to the West it (the Communist party) offered another deal: forget human rights, the Dalai Lama and all that, leave us with our system and we will leave you alone. Together we can create a 'harmonious world' and what's more we will lend you the money to buy our goods."*

Chinese geopolitics is covered under: resources, trade-and-aid, trade deficit/surplus and the RMB (Renminbi) valuation, language and culture and military presence.

Resources: raw materials, energy, manpower, and, critically, water

Raw materials
There is no shortage of publicity about the shortage of raw materials: steel, coal, cement, building materials and so forth. And wherever one looks the hand of China can be seen garnishing these resources to feed into its growing and insatiable building and manufacturing enterprises. China Inc is competing, very successfully, on all fronts and on all continents: Asia, its backyard; Africa, Australia, Latin America, and Canada in North America, full of riches.

There is not one commodity where there is no Chinese organisation at play. It used to export silver, but with the use in photo-voltaic cells in solar panels, it has become an importer. And in one area, that of rare earth elements (*REE*), China - for the present - seems to have a monopoly. These 17 elements are needed in <u>many of today's technologies</u>, from smartphones, to batteries, to catalytic converters and missile systems. Although <u>globally there are more of these metals than say gold</u>, in the past 20 years, China had been mining their deposits in Mongolia at such a low cost that many existing miners have shut shop. Only to discover that in 2009, the need is for 134,000 tons but with only 124,000 being mined, the deficit coming from stocks. Although China has 34% of the REEs, it has cornered over 95% of the production.

The <u>EU initiated a study</u> of potential shortage of 49 raw materials including rare earths, precious metal such as cobalt and lithium and, of course uranium plus water. The US is naturally exhorting its miners to restart operations urgently. In about four years, this shortage and monopoly should ease. But the question is: *"What else and where else will a resource shortage emerge?"*

In September 2010, China refused Japan an export licence. The refusal comes amidst rising tensions between China and Japan over a disputed collection of islands in the East China Sea. To some, that is playing geopolitics. This refusal has caused <u>Toyota to form a rare earths team</u>. Each Prius needs, for example, 25 pounds of lanthanum in its nickel-metal hydride battery.

Deep sea resource exploration and extraction is next on the agenda. China sent three scientists to the bottom of the South China Sea in the summer of 2010. They descended more than 3 km in a craft the size of a small truck. Next year the craft, *Jiaolong* (named after a mythical sea dragon), will attempt 5 km and 7km in 2012. The purpose is to lay the foundation for deep sea resource survey and - later - extraction.

Energy

By energy we mean mainly coal, oil, and uranium, as China has an abundance of <u>wind and has become the world leader of solar power</u>, supplying both its own growing needs as well as becoming a leading exporter of photo voltaic panels. Most of China's electricity is produced from fossil fuels (70% from coal, 2% from oil, 1% from gas in 2011) and hydropower (21%). Other renewables account for only 5.5%.

Coal: Although China has vast coal deposits and is the world's largest producer (3.5bn tons in 2011), its needs surpass its own output as coal is needed both for power and for steel making, so it became a <u>major</u>

importer at over 177m tons in 2011 and rising. South Africa and Australia are the main suppliers.

Oil & gas is in short supply as China is increasingly becoming a private car nation. Apparently, in August 2010, Chinese citizens bought around 55% more cars than they did a year ago! Such is the growth of private car ownership that one article said 45% of Chinese car owners have never had to change tyres, their cars being less than 2-3 years old. China has surpassed the US for sales of new passenger cars. Chinese oil companies are involved either as partners or customers around the world, taking stakes in many blocs and investing in some national oil companies such as Petrobras, the Brazilian oil company who was provided with $10bn loan from a Chinese bank in February 2010. China is building a 7,000km gas pipeline to move gas from Turkmenistan via Uzbekistan and Kazakhstan.

Uranium is needed badly by China which has 15 installations in operation in 2012 and 24 being built with many more planned, installing more nuclear power plants than any other country. For instance it provided a $95m loan to Niger (second largest uranium producer after Canada) to expand its uranium mines in 2009.

Manpower
Although there is no surplus labour nor a shortage, with such a huge workforce there is always some flexibility. Consequently, for many infrastructure and plant construction projects funded by aid or FDI, Chinese labourers are much in evidence throughout Africa. In most cases they are welcome and their know-how is appreciated as projects tend to be jointly staffed and knowledge transfer takes place. However, from time to time, if the local employment situation becomes desperate, anger is sometimes taken out on Chinese workers, occasionally resulting in violence, which unfortunately is rising in some African countries.

Water
Professor Sarah Slaughter of MIT warned in 2008 that 'water is the next oil', in terms of scarcity and role in geopolitics. As we noted in our web page on greening of China, China is carrying out major hydro projects that will dwarf the Three Gorges Dam, including a north-south canal that may have both good and unplanned bad consequences. But the problem lies

in the fact that the head waters of many of the SE Asian rivers start in the Himalayas or the Tibetan plateau. So far water sharing has not become a major issue. But it is taking up more and more space in the media. Unless countries start to invest in water desalination and other conservation plans, conflict will be a matter of time, especially with continuing climate warming reducing glacier cover.

Trade-and-aid

China plays a very astute game of trade where possible and aid where necessary. In terms of trade, once again, it invests when it is advantageous to do so (and is permitted to - eg the US vetoed the now infamous offer by CNOOC to buy Unocal) and it enters into ordinary purchase contracts when appropriate. Unlike Western powers, aid does not come with political strings. Aid is transparent as a quid-pro-quo prepayment for something, usually a natural resource.

In its imperial past, tribute from *neighbouring countries* it declined to conquer was the means of both establishing supremacy and also increasing its prosperity. As one political commentator said: the new Chinese 'empire' thrives on trade rather than tribute. Burma, Thailand (supplies China with rice and rubber), Laos, Cambodia (China helped build a 140 mile railway at £140m as part of a trans Asian railway system - more later) and, to a degree, Vietnam, Malaysia, Indonesia (supplier of natural gas and timber), less so the Philippines, Taiwan, South Korea (who sells more to China than US, and has opened 1,000s of factories in China, like Taiwan and Japan and western nations), Japan and even India are trading with China as never before. And one mustn't forget Australia with its vast cache of minerals. And, to India's great concern, China is working with Pakistan on ports, oil pipelines, railroads and even a naval base for Chinese warships; ostensibly to patrol the pirate infested waters of the Arabian Gulf.

Africa is where China is most active. There are between 750,000 and 1m Chinese in Africa, and nearly 1,000 Chinese companies, big and small, mostly since the late 70s-80s. Chinese firms have built prestige projects like national sports stadia, parliament buildings, highways and a 1,100 mile railway across Tanzania to carrying landlocked Zambian copper to Dar es Salaam, along with other goods, of course. This project took 50,000 Chinese workers and engineers and £500m; no small investment.

Africa is blessed with many natural resources: 98% of world's Chromium, 90% of cobalt and platinum, 64% of manganese, 50% of gold, 33% of uranium, more oil than North America, and possibly 40% of world's hydroelectric power. So it was a natural magnet for China. Africa is supplying a third of China's oil needs, with Angola already overtaking Saudi Arabia.

And more due to self-interest than globalisation ambitions, China has essentially filled the semi-vacuum left by ex-colonials who departed. China decided trade rather than aid would help the continent to attain affluence, thereby providing another market for China's manufactured goods. Aid, according to many economists, has not and will not work. China, by contrast, puts trade first and, where necessary, has supplemented it with aid. The significant difference is that there are no ideological strings attached, no demand for 'human rights', 'transparency', democratic elections' or whatever, much to Western annoyance and great disadvantage. This policy is consistent with China's insistence that no country should interfere with another's internal policies and practices. If the goods, services and terms are right, a deal is struck. In 1999, Afro-Sino trade was around $9bn; today it is well over $100bn, second only to US-Afro trade, ahead of France and Britain. Chinese FDI is also substantial. Again the difference is a 10 to 30 year planning cycle for Chinese enterprises as opposed to western companies' 3 to 5 year cycle.

China has been engaged in a kind of 'health diplomacy' with Africa since the 1960s. Health-care development and medical assistance have been one of the main successful areas of cooperation. Between the early 1960s and 2005, more than 15,000 Chinese doctors have been sent to more than 47 (of 53) African countries. The medical teams, known as *yiliaodui*, have treated more than 170 million patients during that period.

In 2001, the member nations of G8, formed the United Nations-backed Global Fund to Fight AIDS, Tuberculosis and Malaria with an initial budget of $10 billion. In 2007, another additional $1.1 billion was approved in China, of which 66% was dedicated to Africa. In September of the same year, China promised the Republic of the Congo to build 31 hospital units and other 145 smaller health care centres, a project due to be completed in March 2010.

When all is said and done, it should be noted that the Chinese per capita GDP is c$5,434 and that of Africa is c$2,500. Case of one set of poor people helping another with mutual self-interest. As President

Festus Mogae of Botswana said:*"China treats us as equals, while the West treats us as former subjects."* When Western powers criticise China, its rebuttal is *"Why after centuries of interaction including colonialism, is Africa so backward and poor? What did you do that was right for Africa?"* At the grass roots level however, there is some resentment of unfair competition and resource grabbing. In an article in <u>Management Today, January 2011</u>, one local observer said *"It has taken us 100s of years to shake off the west, and now all we gain is the east".* Nevertheless, some economists think that China has helped Africa to reach an economic tipping point, a point of no return, turning what has been a vicious cycle into a virtual cycle. Time will tell.

Rest of the World?

Guess what, China has not been idle anywhere. Resources are chased wherever they occur, Canada, Russia, Australia, and Latin America; and from investing in oil and minerals, China is now investing in anything that seems to make sense. This is partly driven by the realisation that, sooner rather than later, over half the treasure chest of $2 trillion trade surplus in US dollars treasury bonds is at risk as gradually the world moves off the $ standard as it did off the gold standard in the past, and as the RMB appreciates either due to 'natural economic' causes or due to pressure from the US. So the Chinese sovereign funds are incessantly searching for decent investments, even taking risks from time to time, a sign of the maturity of the investors in those funds.

Russia is finding that with a large proportion of its raw materials in Siberia, it is far cheaper to sell and ship them to China than to anyone else. In addition, Chinese consumer goods are relatively cheap and of quality to be imported and transported to the far eastern provinces including an oil pipe due for service in 2012. By then a quarter of Russia's crude will be headed east. Surprisingly, Chinese firms have rented vast tracts of vacant agricultural land and encouraging

Chinese farmers to toil there as seasonal labour. Another set of win-win situations, causing many border communities to learn Mandarin along with Russian, of course. Nevertheless, there is some nervousness in Moscow as it realises that the three north eastern provinces of China has c100 million people against some 7 million living in Eastern Siberia.

Latin America is not immune to the Chinese RMB. With the gradual decline of American influence (at one time supporting many right-wing military dictators) Sino-Latin American trade - that increased from $10bn pa in 2000 to $120bn in 2009 - is beginning to approach that of US trade and in the case of Brazil and some other countries, exceed it, causing much anxiety in the Congress and Senate.

Transport initiatives

In addition to investments in banks, industrial firms, China is backing *major transport projects* all over the world, realising that if it has gained the right to certain minerals, they have to get it to a port and thence to China. Also, it is the prime instigator for two trans-Asian railways. One roughly east-west and the other north-south. A *new Oriental Express!*

Passengers could one day be travelling from London to Beijing in a little over a day on trains travelling almost as fast as aeroplanes. China is in negotiations to build a 2,000 mile high-speed rail network to India and Europe with trains capable of travelling at over 200mph within the next ten years. Trains would also travel to Singapore, India and Pakistan - and this is just the first phase. In July 2011, a cargo train loaded with Chinese products travelled from Chongqing to Duisburg, Germany, taking some 13 days and 11,000 km. This compares with 36 days by container ship, and would be cheaper, without the threat of Somalian pirates to boot. The plan is for one such train to leave each day.

A second line would head to Germany via Russia (routes yet undecided), and a third line would extend south from China to connect Vietnam, Thailand, Burma and Malaysia. Further phases could link with the Middle East and, who knows, via Egypt to Africa some day. If and when that happens, the golden age of rail will be back, overturning a very brief age of flight.

For China, it is all about shortening supply lines and reducing their costs. For the countries at the other end of the line it will be a cheaper way to deliver resources and a quicker and cheaper way to receive goods from China. Most would consider this to be a win-win situation. Economic historians believe that railways in the 19th century helped to unify Germany and Italy, and accelerated the development of the USA. Perhaps these new railways will do so for a more globally-enmeshed world of the 21st century.

Civil engineer to the world

In addition to numerous projects in Africa, in Brazil, China is building a gigantic pier at Acu Port to speed up loading of raw materials outbound and manufactured goods inbound. And in the United States, China is completing work on the San Francisco-Oakland Bay Bridge. The steel structures are being built in China and shipped 10,000 km yet saving the authorities $400m.

Trade surplus-deficit and the Renminbi (RMB) valuation

China's cumulative trade surplus of $2 trillion has become an increasing embarrassment for both China and the US (who has a trade deficit to match). This imbalance is not helped by the valuation of the RMB which is controlled. Although the US authorities scream aloud that the RMB should be valued much higher, the reality is that if it was valued much higher there will be two draconian effects: the re-emergence of inflation as a problem for the developed nations and the continuing devaluation of the US dollar that, eventually, will lead it to cease being the exchange currency for most countries and industries. The latter is inevitable, to be replaced (probably) by a basket of currencies. The former is avoidable.

In the background the RMB is gradually being internationalised. Some deals are now transacted in RMB rather than the ubiquitous 'almighty' US dollar. Given China's current policy of currency exchange control, these deals are not subject to forex volatility and are seen to be a better deal. Hong Kong and Singapore are in on the act and in China; Kunming is aiming to lead as the financial hub in Sino-SE Asian trading. In January 2012, Mr George Osborne, UK Chancellor of the Exchequer, gained agreement with Hong Kong to extend its RMB trading hours, so London can get in on the action. This presages London becoming the first RMB trading centre outside of China (and Hong Kong). This will be good for both the UK and China, as it seeks to gradually internationalise the RMB. In the meantime, China and Russia are discussing trading in each others' currencies bypassing the US dollar.

To the credit of the G20 meeting in October 2010, although calls were made to manage surpluses-deficits, no artificial ceiling was imposed - which would, in all probability not worked anyway. And the increase in voting rights at the IMF for China and other BRIC countries was also a good move in the right direction of recognising the increasing economic power of these nations.

A little noticed Chinese law is that of <u>minimum wage</u> which was enacted in 1994 to ensure that low-paid workers have enough to live on. In January 2011, all provinces had to increase minimum wage by 22.8% during 2011. In effect this is tantamount to revaluing the currency upward, as wages, sooner or later, winds its way into export prices.

Chinese culture and language

For centuries, China thought that its own culture and language was all it needed. The shocks of the 19th and early 20th century put paid to that misconception. Ironically, in the 21st century, the world and his uncle are trying to learn Mandarin to further its chances of success in an increasingly G2 world; and to understand the basics of Chinese culture, as a by-product. In July 2011, Sweden wants to offer Chinese as an option to all schools.

China, initially diffident about this voluntary initiative, has taken the movement to heart firstly with the establishment of the <u>Confucius Institutes</u>; and more recently by forming bi-lateral agreements to supply native-speaking Chinese language teachers. China established its first Confucius Institute abroad at the end of 2004. By the June 2009, 282 Confucius Institutes and 272 Confucius Classrooms had been established in 83 countries and regions around the world. For Britons, the Confucius Institutes should be no surprise, the <u>British Council</u> having been around for well over 80 years and operates in over 100 countries. The US used to operate a more overtly American-PR <u>US Information Agency</u> formed by President Eisenhower but more or less disbanded in 1999. In Hungary, there is a bi-lingual <u>Hungarian-Chinese school</u> opened in 2004 and initially attracting mostly Chinese pupils. But it now has 40% Hungarian kids out of 230.

Military presence

China is at pains to act as a 'good citizen' contributing peace-keeping troops, to providing warships to patrol the pirate infested waters off Somalia. As of late 2012 there were 2,150 Chinese military and police personnel supporting the United Nations in 10 countries, including Sudan and Haiti. China has sent small PLA mine-clearing operations to

Iraq and Afghanistan but otherwise has tried to stay clear of military operations in those countries while positioning itself to take advantage of resources and economic benefits offered there.

China is beginning to think of <u>military bases abroad</u>. So far, these have been minor establishments along 'choke points' in its trade routes, either for in-coming oil, coal and iron ore or out-going routes for its container ships. But as one observer put it: *"China is merely following in the footsteps of other major global powers who established military bases abroad to secure their interests. The sooner the world acknowledges this, the better it will be for global stability."* - <u>Harsh V. Pant</u> teaches at King's College, London, and is a visiting fellow at the Center for the Advanced Study of India, University of Pennsylvania.

Despite the 'natural' behaviour of China some neighbours, such as Japan and India, are far from reassured.

To set China's <u>military spend in context</u>: the US military budget in 2011 was c$711bn, bigger than that of all the other countries put together. No wonder the US is treated as the global policeman!

China's was c$143bn including internal paramilitary expenditure, larger than most Euro countries of around $40 to $65bn. It has 2.3m personnel. Note that in early 2011, Obama has asked DOD to reduce the budget to $400bn.

But China is slowly progressing. In January 2011, it launched a prototype J20 stealth fighter, which came as a surprise to Mr Robert Gates, just as he was meeting his Chinese counterpart to try and defuse tensions. Message written in the skies, indeed. And in late 2012, aircraft were landing and taking off its first aircraft carrier.

In May 2011, China admitted it has set up a 30-strong unit of cyber warriors named the Blue Army whose stated purpose is to detect and ward attacks on China. This information seemed to confirm fears amongst many western powers that China is hacking into their military and civilian networks.

By contrast, India's annual military budget in 2011 was $49bn only.

China is wooing everybody

Up to the beginning of the 20th century, China was very reclusive. It deemed itself self-sufficient, not needing anything from anyone else. China in the 21st century seems to have turned itself 180 degrees and is seeking to network and collaborate with everyone. The list of over 100 countries below has been compiled during 2012 from on-line articles in China Daily and Xinhua News. They are countries that either sent senior leaders to China or to which China sent senior leaders (often the Prime Minister) to discuss and agree collaboration, or with whom China forged or renewed some significant treaty or alliance.

In other words, China is not leaving matters to chance but taking proactive action. Maybe the Chinese leaders have read and internalised Dale Carnegie's *How to Win Friends and Influence People*.

On the other hand, maybe China has heard of the saying: *"Keep your friends close, but keep your enemies closer"* and since everyone can at some time be a friend or a foe, China wants to keep close to everyone.

By the way, if your country is not one of those listed, either I missed an article OR you better start worrying.

- December 2012: Mexico, Bolivia, India; New Zealand; USA; Cuba; Kazakhstan; Russia, Iran, Azerbaijan, Latvia; South Africa; Bahrain; Armenia

- November 2012: Nepal, Laos, Pakistan, Maldives, Bangladesh; Cambodia; Luxembourg; Russia; Palestine; Spain; Tajikistan; Benin; Surinam; Italy; Kazakhstan; Kyrgyzstan; Germany

- October 2012: Colombia; The Netherlands; New Zealand; Maldives; Cambodia; Bangladesh; Philippine; Vietnam; Laos; Poland; Romania; Croatia; Moldavia

- September 2012: Vietnam, Russia, Singapore; Myanmar; Malaysia; Turkmenistan; Canada; Cambodia, Sudan, Algeria; France

- August 2012: Bulgaria; Ghana; Taiwan; Indonesia; Brunei; Malaysia; Croatia; Philippines; Egypt; Germany; South Korea; New Zealand; Congo; India; Iran, Myanmar, Sri Lanka, Fiji; Montenegro; Cambodia; Burundi

- July 2012: Cuba; Slovenia; Israel; South Korea; Malaysia; Niger; South Africa; Egypt; Ivory Coast; Equatorial Guinea; Niger; Nepal

- June 2012: Belarus; Georgia: Afghanistan; Myanmar; Laos, Cambodia, Malaysia, Russia; Denmark; Sri Lanka; Belgium; Ethiopia; South Korea; Singapore; Brazil; Congo; Uruguay; Argentina; Mozambique, South Africa, Zimbabwe; Argentina; Poland; Chile;

- May 2012: Kyrgyzstan, Tajikistan, Kazakhstan, Turkmenistan and Uzbekistan; Taiwan; USA, Arab League, Colombia; Japan, South

Korea, Romania, New Zealand, Australia; Croatia; Netherlands; Luxembourg; Brazil; East Timor; Singapore; Kenya; Turkey.

- April 2012: Kazakhstan, Britain, Cyprus, Brunei, Premier Wen visit: Iceland, Sweden, Germany, Poland; Thailand, Japan, North Korea, Timor-L'este, Colombia, South Sudan, Indonesia, VP Li Keqiang, presumed Premier-to-be, visited: Russia, Hungary, Belgium, EU, Central & East Euro states, Malawi, Malaysia, Zambia, South Korea.
- March 2012: Britain, France, Italy, UAE, Albania, Angola, Kenya, Israel, Egypt, Brazil, Venezuela, Turkey, Indonesia, South Korea, South Africa, Japan, Cambodia, Taiwan, Ireland, Russia and India.
- February 2012: VP Xi Jinping, presumed President-to-be, visited US; Canada, Australia, Turkey; Taiwan; Myanmar.
- January 2012: Ivory Coast, Pakistan, Germany, Libya, Sudan, Nepal, Saudi Arabia, Kazakhstan; Vietnam; Chile.

6 PROGNOSIS

Prognosis is the assessment or prediction (in the sense of a best educated guess) of the future course of the development, outcome, or progress of a condition or phenomenon, based on a careful diagnosis of the case.

(From http://tinyurl.com/blnalpe).

As one wag said *"predicting is very difficult, especially where the future is concerned"*.

To look ahead 25 years is very daunting. Just think back 25 years to 1986 - the snippets below were mainly from: The Year 1988 from *The People History*

- *USA* was number 1, and the **USSR** was number 2, in power if not in GDP terms. It will be another year before the fall of the Berlin Wall and the subsequent breakup of the USSR; and 13 years before the term BRIC is invented, to include Russia
- *China* was eight years into the economic reform initiated by Deng Xiaoping; and a year before the infamous Tiananmen Incident
- *India* had Rajiv Gandhi as its Premier, four years after his mother Indira Gandhi was assassinated by her Sikh bodyguards; and three years before he himself was assassinated by a female 'Tamil Tiger'.
- *Benazir Bhutto* is elected to be Prime Minister of Pakistan (also assassinated in 2007)
- After 8 years and 1.5 million dead the *Iran -- Iraq war ends*
- Suspected *Libyan terrorist bomb explodes on Pan Am jet over Lockerbie* in Scotland on December 21 killing all 259 on board and 11 on the ground

- Soviet *Red Army withdraws from Afghanistan.*
- *Yasser Arafat* is invited to address the U.N. General Assembly
- *Technology:*
  - *First transatlantic fiber optic cable* laid able to carry 40,000 telephone calls simultaneously
  - Stephen Hawking publishes *"A Brief History Of Time"*
  - The first major *computer virus* infects computers connected to the Internet.
  - The *Hubble Space Telescope* is put into operation
  - The *US Stealth Bomber* is unveiled
  - The antidepressant *Prozac* introduced which quickly became the market leader for treating depression.

It is foolhardy for anyone to try and predict 25 years on. So we will try and predict where we can and where we cannot, we will try and identify the major uncertainties that lie ahead for China and for India. To that end we have read a lot and tried to compile likely scenarios. To paraphrase Sir Isaac Newton, *"If I seem to be seeing so far, it is only because I stand on the shoulders of giants."* One of the giants, from whom we have borrowed extensively for this section, is the Economist (the world in 2036 and subsequent annual previews). We have acknowledged our sources and apologies if we omitted anyone inadvertently.

Economically, Jim O'Neill, Goldman Sachs (inventor of the term BRIC) said in The Economist's *'The World in 2011'* that China is likely to overtake the US by 2027. Since then, OECD has shortened it to 2016! Note that OECD is using the less popular *'purchasing power parity'* GDP rather than the more common *'nominal'* GDP.

At present, China is no 2 after the US in GDP terms (since 2010). India is still lagging behind at no 10 (2011). Both nations have pulled 100s of millions out of poverty, with China having a distinct edge. But neither China nor India is amongst the top 100 in GDP per capita terms. China has invested heavily in *infrastructure* and *plant*, and kicked off a new five-year plan in 2011 with more than $1tr allocated to infrastructure. Not to be beaten, India tried but failed to spend the remaining funds allocated to its $500bn infrastructure budget for the five years to March 2012. Private financiers will augment lending to the infrastructure sector from $2bn in 2010 to $9bn in 2013 and will help developers and contractors access these funds.

By the way, for non-historians, China and India between them was estimated to cover 50% of the world's GDP up to c200 years ago. So, if the predictions come true, future historians will look at the last 200 years as an aberration.

China has developed a very *modern army* but lacks substantial experience. By contrast, although India's army is under-funded in comparison, it not only has had experience fighting several major wars with Pakistan, its military tradition goes back to both British India days when Indian troops fought in both World Wars under the Union Jack and pre-Raj era when fighting the British with some success.

Both have *problems with neighbors*: India with Pakistan and to a degree with China; China with many of its neighbors both on land and increasingly across resource-rich seas.

Both have *internal problems*: India with its Muslim minority becoming polarized with both global movements and Pakistan-instigated unrest caused by the continuing Kashmiri issue, as well as with the Naxalites, Maoist dissidents; China with two of its three major minorities: Tibetans and Uighurs (fortunately the Mongolian minority seems to be relaxed about its well-being).

India is the world's *largest democracy* - though de facto single-party. China is the world's *largest autocracy*, but a very successful one at that.

India's *population* is very young and even by 2050 youth will predominate. China, with its one-child policy, is beginning to become concerned that *"it will become old before it becomes rich"*.

India has well-established and (largely) *transparent institutions*, many the legacy of British rule. China, by contrast, is still coming to terms with the 'rule of law' (as opposed to dictat by local and national party cadres).

One of the assertions made by many economists and other commentators including <u>Raghav Bahl</u> in his excellent book *Superpower? The Amazing Race between China's Hare and India's Tortoise* - is that although China is predicted to overtake the US as the world's first economy - perhaps before 2038 - India will overtake China well before the end of this century.

We will examine the basis for these assertions and make our own predictions. The remaining web pages will comprise of - by 2038:

- Will China and India be superpowers?
- How close will India be economically?
- What will be China's position and relationship with the 'rest of the world'?
- What are the likely political pitfalls for China and for India?

- What will be social, cultural and - most important - demographic changes?
- How well will China and India have innovated?

6.1   Will China be a superpower by 2038?

A superpower is a state with a dominant position in the international affairs which has the ability to influence events and its own interests and project power on a worldwide scale to protect those interests. A superpower is traditionally to be one step higher than a great power. Until the breakup of the Soviet Union there were two superpowers. At present there is only one - the USA. *(Adapted from Wikipedia).*

The question therefore is whether both China and India will be more powerful than any other nation apart from the US by 2038. Our educated guess is that China probably will be at or nearly at the level of the US, but India will only be a 'great' power by then, alongside Japan, Germany and perhaps Russia.

Superpower China

The reason for our prediction about China is that it is already well on its way to becoming a superpower: in terms of economics - there is already talked of a G2, military development and through its seemingly ubiquitous deals with most nations across all continents. Each deal may seem innocuous and 'natural' - for resources, for technology know-how, to build infrastructure or factories; and to provide financial backing to debt-ridden Euro states. But taken together, they are both a projection of power, in the sense of *"we can do it and you need us more than we need you"* as well as in sowing the seeds for future returns. We know that nations, like people, can be forgetful. But a memory can nevertheless be refreshed, and a happy memory can often stand one in good stead. In gambling, the term is `calling in or cashing in the chips'` when needed.

The reason for our prediction about India becoming a great power but not a superpower by 2038 is that India is lagging behind in all three areas: the economy (more later), the military, and in international deals. Yes, Indian firms are making deals. But because they are done individually without a national strategy, they make business sense to the Indian firm and, hopefully, to its partner, but often do not further the interests of India as a nation. For each Indian deal, there must be a dozen equivalent Chinese deals. Also, some Chinese deals are 'unique' in that once done, there is little opportunity for a second-comer to get a look in. So, if China has helped a land-locked African nation to build a backbone road or rail network, all a second party (be it a commercial or a national entity) can do is to flesh it out, with reduced publicity and reward.

As China is slowly flexing its muscle, America is gradually relaxing: it consciously decided to take a back seat in the Libyan situation, purposely letting NATO take a lead - unheard of even five years ago. That is one of the unintended consequences of wars in Iraq and Afghanistan; and - indirectly, of the US-led banking crisis. Obama has also decided to reduce the US military presence in Europe by 25% in 2015. However, towards the end of 2011, beginning of 2012, when announcing cuts in defense spending, Obama made clear, the Pacific will be a centre of focus, hinting ever so clearly that it will not tolerate Chinese domination that worries several of its neighbor who have mutually incompatible claims to the sea around them, deemed to contain untold oil and gas reserves.

In a surprise move, China staged a successful test flight of a military spacecraft to rival the US's secret X-37B. The announcement came just before the US Defense Secretary Robert Gate's visit to China in January 2011 to mark the final step towards resumption of military relationships with China since a rift over us arms sales to Taiwan. Call it timing.

In the civilian aerospace field, China is about to complete its satellite set to provide GPS so that it is not dependent on the US or European systems.

In _Why the West Rules - for now_, Ian Morris convincingly argues that just as Britain could not stop America's rise, neither can America stop China's ascendancy.

G2?

Having a G2 is no bad thing. We would not have had the recent fiascos like Iraq and Afghanistan with essentially a G1 and - possibly - avoided the excesses of the credit crisis (though some analysts blame the Chinese 'cheap' products and propensity for absorbing US debt for making money so cheap it led to greedy bankers overextending themselves, but that is another story). This is especially so, as unlike the previous G2 of protagonists, the USA and the USSR, we will have two highly interdependent G2, albeit one is the banker and supplier and the other the debtor and customer. As someone said, if you owe the bank a $100, it is your problem. But if you owe the bank $1 trillion, it becomes the banker's problem!

China is keenly mindful of its dependency on the US dollar. In recent years it has done two things to mitigate against this risk. Firstly, from 90%, it is estimated that only 60% of the $1 trillion surplus is denominated in US dollars. When President Hu in June 2011 declared China will continue to support the Euro despite the Greek debt crisis, he was only stating what was and is happening. The second action is that China's various sovereign funds are buying into foreign companies, either by outright takeover or by JVs. Initially, these were in energy or raw materials, but increasingly, the funds are playing where there is money to be made, regardless of sector.

Late in 2010, the IMF initiated a set or sweeping reforms. One of these is to recognize China's economic strength and consequently China will leapfrog Germany, France and Britain to be IMF's third most powerful member after the US and Japan. India will also be granted more authority.

More important than anything else is how the IMF is viewing national debt. Largely ignored, this is coming to the fore with S&P threatening to downgrade the US rating because of not only its deficit and national debt, but because of the lack of any sign that politicians in Washington seem to have any desire to curb the deficit and to plan to reduce the debt. Until recently, nations in surplus were under scrutiny. There is now increasing recognition that it takes two hands to clap and deficit nations are beginning to be called to reform. It is increasingly clear the current state of deficit/surplus cannot go on for much longer.

Then in August 2011, the unthinkable happened, the US credit rating was downgraded from triple A despite the debt ceiling being raised above the current astronomical £14.3 trillion by $2.5 trillion

News on August 6, 2011 offers a big indicator of the shifting economic power balance between China and the US. Xinhua, the Chinese state news agency, said this in a statement: *"China, the largest creditor of the world's sole superpower, has every right now to demand the United States to address its structural debt problems and ensure the safety of China's dollar assets. To cure its addiction to debts, the United States has to re-establish the common sense principle that one should live within its means. It should also stop its old practice of letting its domestic electoral politics take the global economy hostage and rely on the deep pockets of major surplus countries to make up for its perennial deficits."*

The dollar is waning slowly as the world's reserve currency and the currency of exchange. The Chinese Yuan is slowly gaining ground as the currency of exchange amongst its top trading partners outside of the US and Europe. But to become an alternative to the dollar, it must first become an international fully convertible currency allowed to float freely. China has called for a review of a new stable reserve currency. In all probability this will be based on a 'basket of currencies', such as the US dollar, the Euro, the RMB and perhaps some other currencies.

Of course, as historians sometimes remind us, Rome did not fall in a day or even a year but over centuries to at least when <u>Romulus Augustus</u>, the last <u>Emperor</u> of the <u>Western Roman Empire</u>, was deposed by <u>Odoacer</u>, a Germanic chieftain. By then it had lasted a millennium. The British Empire from the founding of the East India Company to the end of WWII only lasted a third of a millennium. So will the US ascendancy last under a century, from the end of WWII to 2038? And will they in 2038 remember August 2011 as the beginning of the end of American supremacy?

6.2   How close will India be by 2038?

If current trends continue, then by 2038, India will be champing at the heels of China. The world will be led by a G2, with a possible G3 in the wings. China is variously predicted to overtake the US in nominal GDP terms in the next 15 to 25 years. And many predict that India will overtake firstly, the US, in another 15 to 25 years; and secondly, China in a further 15 to 25 years. In other words they predict that China's economic leadership will last no more than three to five decades and by the end of the 21st century the ranking will be India, China, and America. It should be noted that up to 1978 India's GDP was ahead of China's and, according to the IMF; <u>India's growth in 2010 </u>was slightly higher than China's.

Analysts who predict that India will beat China sooner rather than later base their views on the following:
o   *Demographics:* India has a growing young population
o   *Democracy:* India follows parliamentary democracy; China follows one-party rule

o *The rule of law:* India is more transparent and conforms to a recognisable western model; China is largely opaque and follows its own model

o *Language:* more Indians are English fluent than Chinese

o *Capitalism:* Indian versus Chinese.

We discuss each of these factors. We also discuss factors that militate against India overtaking China any time soon. A simple indicator is that of the World Economic Forum <u>competitiveness indicator</u>. China improved from 34 in rank in 2007 to 27 in 2011, while India dropped from 48 to 51. These include:

o *Infrastructure:* India lags behind and will take decades to catch up

o *Economic disparity:* whereas Chinese economic growth seems to have percolated down to the masses, India's record so far is that the poor have not benefited as much. This disparity is in terms of both urban versus rural and upper versus lower castes, not to mention the purported illegal classification of out-caste.

o *Literacy and skills:* China decided decades ago that everyone, farmers included need to be educated. As a result, literacy and numeracy is practically universal at 93%. By contrast India's workforce is estimated to be only 66% literate.

o *Political tensions :* although both countries have serious political tensions, India has lurking across the 'red corridor' an insurgency that may erupt into a major revolution, the likes of which one can only imagine as that of the Russian or Chinese revolution.

o *Corruption:* while both China and India suffer from corruption - both are in the mid ranges by country according to Transparency International - the difference is that China tries to do something about it, whereas India seems to be more complacent.

o *Peasants and women:* whereas China, since Liberation in 1949 has steadily removed barriers for equality between the rural and urban populations and between women and men, this is far from so in India.

Factors favouring India

The factors that favor India are its demographics, democracy and rule of law, language (English), and capitalism.

Demographics

India, like many developing nations, has more young people than old with 65% under 35 years of age (median age 25) and that ratio is increasing. In times past this would have been a disadvantage. But with enough food and jobs (at least for now), this is an advantage. In contrast, having adopted a one-child policy for decades which is slowly being eased, China, like Japan and the developed nations, the population is ageing - median age 34. The expression 'getting old before getting rich' is truly applicable to China, for despite its nominal GDP being second only to the US, the per capita GDP is amongst those of poor developing nations. India is at the same level at present. But with accelerated growth and assuming its belated investment in infrastructure takes, it will, in due course, speed ahead of China.

Note, however, that population is a two-edged sword. If handled properly, it is an advantage. But if food and or water supply falls short and a poor infrastructure prevents surplus areas supplying those in deficit, could soon become a major disadvantage.

Of all the factors favouring India over China in the medium term, demographics is the least debatable.

Democracy and the Rule of Law

Democracy is inefficient: a <u>bumpier but freer road</u>. If India was to undertake a dam akin to the Three Gorges, it would still be in the planning stage, if not still in the public consultation stage. However, let's not forget that after the Second World War, Germany and Japan made huge leaps forward, despite being democracies. On the other hand, if someone like Mao were to take over the Chinese leadership again, with support of the Red Army, who can or will stop him? It is no good saying *"that is most unlikely."*

Thanks to democracy, West Bengal overturned its Communist Party majority in May 2011 after three decades. The winner is *Mamata Banerjee*, a woman politician. At the same time, the Communists also lost Kerala. In Tamil Nadu, another woman, a former movie star, *Jayalalitha* (who goes by a single name) won.

With true democracy comes the voice of the people. In India, despite holding to obsolete caste and other repressive practices, there are regular protests and demonstrations against such practices, often triggered by some particularly offensive incident, such as the organized rape of a woman because her brother happened to try and elope with a woman of a higher caste. And sometimes these achieve the results intended.

Chinese people also protest and demonstrate. But more often than not, despite travelling all the way to Beijing to petition as they did in Imperial times, their pleas fall on deaf ears, such as the claims of shoddy construction caused by corruption which led to many school buildings collapsing in the Szechuan earthquake in 2008. These petitions subsequently led to the arrest of world famous artist Ai WeiWei in 2011 who joined the cause. Unlike in India, Mr Ai has not been put on trial. He follows many other dissidents arrested and incarcerated without trial. Eventually, following international protests, Ai was released in June 2011 only to face a tax evasion law suit - which he claims is not true.

It should be noted, however, that in many rural areas of India, the voters are not necessarily voting as they choose, but are 'guided' by local leaders and, in some cases, by local landlords and others to whom the farmers are indebted to. Sometimes, whole villages or districts vote unanimously - a rare occurrence if they were voting voluntarily.

Patrick French, in researching for his book *India: A Portrait'*, found that every Indian MP under 30 has in effect 'inherited' a seat from a family member. Not quite as non-representative as the composition of the Chinese people's national assembly, but...

English language

Although the Chinese are catching up, India counts English as one of its national languages. A natural consequence of this is that middle and upper class families tend to send their children to schools where the medium of instruction is English. In some cases these kids know and speak English better than their mother tongue, especially if the family's native tongue is different from that of the city/state they live in which covers all of south India and the east such as Assam and Bengal. Learning a language as one subject amongst many is altogether different from learning all subjects (apart from languages) in English.

As English is the international language for trade and commerce and of many industry sectors such as IT, air transport, pharmaceuticals, diplomacy, and of course multi-national firms, knowing English intuitively is a tremendous advantage compared to knowing it as a learned school subject. They say, your real mother tongue is the one you dream in, and for many educated Indians that is exactly so. However, since 2001, English has become compulsory in Chinese schools from the age of around 9. This means that by now (2011), all school leavers will be able to at least read English, even if they cannot quite speak it fluently. So, by 2038, the language advantage will have been eroded.

However, in many countries, partly encouraged by the formation of Confucius Institutes, more and more children are being enrolled in Chinese language lessons. Within a couple of generations, speaking English may be far less an advantage than speaking Mandarin.

Capitalism

Indian capitalism consists both of the internationally recognized form such as practiced by Tata and other global firms that happen to count either India as its home country of Indians as its owners/leaders; and of the local 'mama-papa' indigenous variety' and many more in between. At the grass-roots level, there is probably not much difference between Indian and Chinese capitalism. But once one looks at the larger firms, we immediately see that nearly all Indian firms are privately owned and directed - for example, IndiGo, a young low-cost airline in June 2011 placed the largest single Airbus order for 180 aircraft at $15.6 billion; whereas a majority of larger Chinese firms are either state owned or at least state directed. There is no material difference as long as the state direction is commercially sensible. But if the state decides to direct a firm in a political and non-commercially sensible manner then the results may be detrimental to the customers or staff of the firm.

A particular characteristic of India's capitalism is that many of the large firms are essentially family businesses. They work well in normal circumstances, but sometimes things can go wrong. This happened when Dhirubhai Ambani, founder of Reliance Industries, died and resulted in a long-winded feud between his two sons, Mukesh and Anil, which led to the eventual breakup of Reliance Industries into two independent companies with similar names.

In September 2011, India announced it is setting up a Sovereign Wealth Fund to help finance global acquisition projects in particular of natural resources.

Of the factors favoring India over China, this is the least likely to be a major advantage to India.

Factors against India

Several factors work against India becoming a superpower by 2038. These include infrastructure, economic disparity, skills & literacy, political tensions, corruption and peasants & women.

Infrastructure

India's infrastructure is woefully inadequate. McKinsey estimates that India will need 300GW by 2017 (equivalent of 300 nuclear power stations.) which means that the current pace of installing new power stations need to be increased by between 5 and 10 times. Around 40% of freight is carried by rail in India, despite its legendary railway system. In China and the US rail freight accounts for 50%.

Although economically India is more than a developing nation, its infrastructure is not much ahead of developing nations in Africa. Many African states, with Chinese support either or both in terms of finance and engineering are beginning to look more able to support rapid growth than India. The Economic Intelligence Unit (part of the Economist) recently ranked India 75th out of 82 countries in terms of infrastructure.

For example, Bangalore barely manages to survive its daily traffic jams. It's a good thing that most of the call centre customers are in very different time zones. Gurgaon, a new city 25 km south of New Delhi has grown from practically nothing to the Indian base of many 'household' global firms in 20 years with 1.5 million population. There are 200,000 migrant workers, many as household servants. One estimate is that 500,000 people in Gurgaon are involved in outsourcing. On the surface it is very modern with 26 shopping malls, seven golf courses, luxury shops, modern office blocks and apartment buildings. But there is no city wide sewer or drainage system, reliable electricity or water, parking, decent roads or citywide public transport. Garbage collection is an erstwhile service.

In June 2011, an estimated 18 million tonnes of grain lie exposed to the elements because the government has failed to invest in storage capacity. Storage capacity runs at 50 million tonnes to cover emergencies, another 15 million tonnes is planned but will not be ready for two years.

Tesco, a UK-based retailer is about to expand in India. Kishore Biyani, head of India's biggest retailer, Future Group, warned that Tesco had better invest in bullock carts to supply its planned out-of-town superstores as roads are not good enough for the envisaged volume. This harks back to when Duke of Wellington, then Brigadier Arthur Wellesley, hired huge herds of bullocks to provide an extensive supply chain when he defeated Tipu Sultan. It seems that Indian transport has not changed much in 200 plus years!

China's growth is supported by good infrastructure. India's is despite poor infrastructure. So how does it work? Through private enterprise compensating for poor public service. Offices and apartments have diesel generators and in-house water tanks. Corporations provide private buses or taxis for staff, esp for women working very early or late. Private security outnumbers official police, in Gurgaon by four to one.

India had planned to spend $500bn on infrastructure in the current five-year plan to 2012. Nuclear plants will account for $100bn over 10 years. 80 GWatts (the equivalent of 80 nuclear plants) are under construction. But a recent estimate is that only half will be spent. It is planning to spend $1 trillion to 2017. No one is optimistic that such a sum will actually be spent. Despite producing some 170,000 new engineers pa, many dream of working in IT rather than civil or mechanical engineering. The EIU predicts that by 2014, India's infrastructure will rank 73rd.

India is trying its best to catch up with China in many areas. For example, it formed Indian Ports Global to develop overseas ports along the model of Dubai's DP World. This organization will initially be under India's Shipping Ministry, which is also at the same time developing Indian ports as 90% of Indian import/export is carried by sea. This is both a strategic move as well as a reaction to China building ports in Sri Lanka (Hambantota), Pakistan (Gwadar), Burma (KyaukPhyu) and Bangladesh (Sonadia) - countries India considers within its zone of influence. Shipping Corporation of India is, simultaneously, planning to purchase 100 new ships in the next 10 years.

There is good news too. The 'golden quadrilateral' highway linking Delhi, Bombay, Chennai (Madras) and Calcutta was been completed in October 2010 and is attracting increasing traffic. The Delhi Metro surpassed 2m passengers recently and phase III will extend the lines to 380km and 4m passengers by 2016. It was built on time and to budget. There are 126 domestic airports and internal passenger air traffic grows relentlessly: nearly 25% in 2011 compared to 2010.

Of the factors is India's disfavor, infrastructure is the most critical.

Economic disparity

India has a developed middle class that is growing from an estimated 50 million today to 580 million in 15 years. But the poor, both rural and urban, are not being pulled up as rapidly as in China. Extreme poverty - defined as earning less than $1 per day - is much higher in India than China and dropping slower. Some 400m Indians are still deemed extremely poor. Part of the reason is the caste system, and the second, in villages, is that the landlord / feudal structure has not been eradicated in India as it had been in the early years of the revolution in China. Many farmers are beholden to their landlords, much as it has been for centuries. Even migrating to the city for jobs often depends on loans from the landlord to cover costs. The other effect of the old landlord system is that most of agriculture is in small holdings not prone to major mechanization and productivity gains.

Every year that passes sees more of the Dalits and people from 'tribal' areas move up through reserved education and public sector jobs. One day, caste will no longer be an issue. But not yet. Of the unfavorable factors, caste is probably the least problematic.

Literacy and skills

Despite the statistics about Indian graduates in science and engineering, there is a shortage of skilled labor. The quality is also variable. The best universities including the famous Indian Institutes of Technology are world class, but many others produce graduates good at passing exams but not at real-life jobs. The outsourcing firms tend to run full-time courses for many of their fresh intake to bring them up to adequate levels before assigning them to business activities.

Political tensions

Earlier we mentioned the Red Corridor, a swathe of states from North East to South West which is dominated by insurgents and militants. Around 200 of the 588 districts are affected. In some states, whole districts are 'no go' areas for the police. Only the army or paramilitary police hold any sway at all.

Corruption

Both China and India are perceived to be corrupt. Transparency International places both at around the midpoint amongst nations. The big difference is that China tries to curb it. Hundreds of officials are executed each year. An official report by People's Bank of China (leaked by accident) tells of 10,000 corrupt officials escaping abroad with £80 billion of ill-gotten gains. President Hu, in his address at the 90th Anniversary of the Chinese Communist Party, saw fit to speak out against corruption. In India, it is more muted, although Pratyush Sinha, retired head of India's corruption watchdog said in September 2010 that 30% of his compatriots are 'utterly corrupt'. And an initiative to pass an anti-corruption law in 2011 was passed by the Lokh Sabha (the lower house) but blocked by the Rajya Sabha (the upper house); and the activist morphed into a political party.

Corruption is most common in transactions involving land, public contracts and natural resources. Two ministers are charged with bribery in awarding 2G telecoms licences that may have cost India up to £25bn in lost licence fees. The very stuff that concerns infrastructure, the most serious stumbling block to India's progress.

Matters are changing though. There is a proposal by Kausik Basu, advisor to PM Manmohan Singh that will stop the payer from being sued and go only for the receiver. This way, there will be some encouragement for those not wanting to pay bribes to blow the whistle.

In August 2011, India seemed to be awakening to the detrimental effects of corruption by rallying to the support of Anna Hazare who was on hunger strike, demanding an independent Ombudsman who will be the last call for not only civil servants but also ministers. This has not only aroused the politically alert middle class but even the famous tiffin carries, the 5,000 strong dubbawallahs of Bombay, who deliver 100,000s of office workers with hot lunches prepared by wives or mothers have gone on strike in support; their first in 120 years.

Peasants and women

In China, there is no visible bar to women taking senior roles in government or industry. Admittedly, members of the Central Politburo Standing Committee were and are all men. But in industry, women are as likely to be bosses or owners as men. And there are no structural or institutionalized bars to peasants moving into cities to work or to open businesses in villages and rural areas.

The story in India is very different. There is still the perception that a woman moves from her father's house into her husband's house. Yes, there are a lot of women in IT in Bangalore and Gurgaon. But they are the exceptions rather than the rule.

Even without a one-child policy, there is an estimated imbalance of c1 million girls a year due to female infanticide mainly through illegal abortions. Peasants and the Dalits, as well as tribal people (reflected in the Naxalite insurgency), still find it hard to break into the upward mobile careers, despite 60 years of affirmative action. It was only in 2009 that an act was passed to provide universal, <u>free and compulsory education</u> for all children aged between six and 14. No wonder illiteracy is around 33% (China's is 9%), with only 50% for women. China passed the equivalent of this law 60 years or three generations ago.

The net effect is that India is running with 1/4 of its full human capital. A great self-inflicted drawback.

After infrastructure, this is the second most critical negative factor.

"Ten reasons why India will not and must not become a superpower"

Ramachandra Guha, the renowned Indian historian and author (India after Gandhi), asserts there are ten reasons why India, despite its enormous economic growth, will not become a superpower.

Guha focuses mainly on the internal problems of the 'unique political experiment' *India.* The ten reasons are:
1. Rise of left-wing insurgency in Central and Eastern India (a brutal civil war between the Maoists and the government).
2. Rise of right-wing religious fundamentalism (BJP/RSS).
3. Decline and corruption of the democratic center (particularly the conversion of political parties into family firms).
4. Degradation of public institutions (such as universities, law courts, hospitals, civil services).
5. Growing (spectacular) gap between the rich and the poor.
6. Rapid pace of environmental degradation (air pollution, dead rivers, depletion of groundwater aquifers, disposal of toxic and nuclear waste, etc.).
7. Superficiality of the mainstream media (or "the Indian media's complicit worship of wealth, celebrity and super-stardom") and abandonment of commitment to serious environmental reportage.
8. Political fragmentation and the instability engendered by multiparty coalition governments.
9. Unreconciled borderlands (Kashmir, Nagaland and Manipur).
10. Unstable neighborhood (Pakistan, Bangladesh, Nepal and Sri Lanka).

Conclusion
In the words of Guha: "There are too many fault lines in our society to be a superpower. As a historian I say: 'we are not prepared', as an Indian citizen I say: 'we should not even attempt to'. India should adhere to its constitutional ideals, fight national fires, and heal and harmonize.

6.3 China's relationship with the Rest of the World

Underlying our view expressed in this section is an optimistic assumption that the maritime territorial disputes of 2012 with some six or more of its neighbours will be sorted out in a relatively peaceful and amicable manner within the next year or two.

If current trends continue, then by 2038, most countries will be beholden to China. Some because they will be financially indebted - today's Greece, Portugal and Spain, others because their economic and industrial wellbeing would not have been achieved without Chinese injection of capital or engineering and construction - many African (trade increased by 10 times in a decade to $100bn; most of it in infrastructure projects which has a multiplier effect on economies; eg a 900 mile railway renovation project in Angola) and increasingly Latin America (see sidebar); and some central Asian nations. Yet others because China treated them as equals and traded with them without strings when most Western nations looked upon them as pariahs - Burma, Iran, North Korea and Zimbabwe to name but a few.

Another set of nations will be indirectly grateful because China paved the way for contract manufacturing, and as the so-called China price rises steadily (see sidebar) - wages have increased by up to 30% in the past few years, especially in large factories aimed at mass production' and the Yuan keeps appreciating - and Chinese factories move up the quality chain, these nations start to become the factories of the world - countries such as Indonesia, Malaysia, Philippines, Vietnam, Thailand, Sri Lanka, Turkey and Mexico - as also some ex-Soviet satellites in eastern Europe. This is already happening for certain goods such as textile goods and low-end electronics.

What is not commonly known, according to He Liu Xiaoming, Chinese ambassador to Great Britain, is that China is the largest peacekeeping troop contributor of the UN Security Council, having sent c20,000 peacekeeping personnel on 24 UN missions; that, in addition to trade-aid support to 69 developing countries, it has also sent medical teams of 21,000 doctors and nurses treating 260 million patients in 69.

Negative reactions?

Our perception is that there will be four countries resentful of China's achievements and standing: the USA because of it losing its position as Number 1, by 2038; India, because of its rivalry for the top rank within the 21st century as well as a not quite resolved border dispute; Japan due to long-standing historical envy and enmity; and not forgetting Russia who may be tempted to hark back to the Stalin-Mao era when China was the follower and Russia the leader. However, the reality of China looms large. Oleg Deripaska who runs Rusal the world's biggest aluminium group in June 2011 said he is planning to invest billions of dollars in Siberian hydroelectric plants to supply northern China with power. It is not an altruistic plan but rather one of creating mutual benefit.

There are also potential issues with some of its neighbours due to either diversion of water, such as with Burma and India, or due to contested seas for either fishing or mineral extraction reasons.

In addition, not all African reaction will be positive. Already an estimated 1m Chinese live and work in Africa - not all on large construction or mineral extraction projects. And of those there is resentment that so many jobs, such as 10,000 in construction that could go to Africans are not. Quite different from colonial times when only the 'sahibs' were non-African. Furthermore, there are an estimated 1,000 small traders operating shops and other SMEs. It is not entirely clear whether they are adding or reducing jobs for Africans. It should be noted that unlike Western powers, China regards Africa not as a continent in need of aid, but as a vast continent full of opportunity. (See The _Dragon's Gift:_ Deborah Brautigam.)

In recent years, large tracts of arable land in Africa are being acquired by foreign firms including the Chinese. Most of the land will be used to grow crops. But some are earmarked for biofuel rather than human consumption. This has both a positive and negative effect. Positive as the investment and yield are likely to be substantially higher. Negative, as the produce is more than likely to go abroad, leaving Africans even shorter of food than ever. Land is being bought elsewhere, such as in Australia and South America.

Tom Friedman, NY Times, author of _The World is Flat_, is supposed to have said: _"One of the most unsettling things about the Chinese is not their communism but their capitalism."_

Power struggle between China, India and Japan

In the view of Bill Emmott, ex-editor of The Economist (1993-2006) - *Rivals: How the Power Struggle Between China, India, and Japan Will Shape Our Next Decade* - there will be, hopefully, a three-way balance of power. He sees great parallels between China of recent decades and Japan from the Meiji Restoration to modern times. However, he hopes that the military belligerence of the Japanese during that period will not be repeated by the Chinese, not least (according to Martin Jacques, the author of *When China Rules the World*) because of the invisible but real resumption of a tributary state system with China in the middle - hence Middle Kingdom surrounded by a host of sovereign states paying tribute to China. Nevertheless, Emmott worries that Tibet may prove to be the flash point between China and India.

Additionally, apart from any border dispute, there is inevitability about water dispute. Earlier, we mentioned China's plans to divert water from its wet south to the dry north along three canals. The western most starts in Tibet and if implemented could have severe consequences for India as one of the rivers to be diverted (40 billion cubic metres a year), the Yaluzangbu, is also one of the main sources of the Brahmaputra a main tributary of the Ganges.

How the West was Lost

In the view of Dambisa Moyo, ex-Goldman Sachs, author of *How the West was Lost* there are three significant differences between 'the West' and China that will cause this sea-change to happen within a few decades:

o The Western approach to personal and national wellbeing through debt financing versus the Chinese (and Indian) propensity to save and spend from savings.

o The Western attitude to children as creatures to be pampered and who hanker for instant fame and fortune in entertainment or sport versus the Chinese (and Indian) attitude that children must be educated and steered to seek meaningful and worthwhile careers.

o The Western attitude to individual human rights often to the disbenefit of the greater whole - which we see in the UK in the overly 'liberal' interpretation of the European Human Rights legislation versus the Chinese attitude that the majority needs to be protected, sometimes at the cost of the minority.

China price

China will likely see 'strong' increases in salaries in the five years through 2015 as the nation's supply of labour dwindles and consumers begin to spend more and save less, Credit Suisse Group AG said in a report.

Wages may increase to be equal to 62 percent of China's gross domestic product by 2015 from 50.5 percent in 2011, a team of Credit Suisse analysts led by Vincent Chan and Peggy Chan wrote in a report.

China's leaders said last month that boosting incomes is a major task for the nation in its 12th Five-Year Plan (2011-2015).

---

*China is on track to become **Brazil's No. 1 investor** in 2010 – from* China Daily *- May 2011:*

Just past a port where workers are building a two-mile-long pier to accommodate huge vessels known as Chinamaxes that will transport iron ore for China's ravenous steel industry, past berths for tankers to lug oil to Beijing, a city of factories is sprouting on an island almost twice the size of Manhattan. Many of the structures will be built with Chinese investment: a steel mill, a shipyard, an automobile plant, a factory to manufacture oil and gas equipment.

"They do not want to be perceived as just natural-resource eaters," said Eike Batista, the Brazilian billionaire behind the port project and one of the world's richest men. "To them, it's common sense."

Starting in 2010, China became Brazil's biggest trading partner, replacing the United States.

6.4 Chinese challenges?

Over 25 years anything can happen. So, on this and the next pages we are going to do our best to highlight political pitfalls that could seriously impact the future.

China is in, what mathematicians would call, an unstable equilibrium. It looks stable, but could be tipped over one way or the other depending on how it faces certain challenges. The challenges we envisage are:

o The continuing ability of the Chinese Communist Party (CPC) to retain the loyalty of its citizens.

o   The patience of Chinese 'have nots' in tolerating the rich and party officials in their 'unfair' share of wealth, sometimes through corruption.

o   The ability of the Chinese central government to continue its sway over Tibet and Xinjiang.

o   The continuing smooth transition of one cohort of senior Chinese leaders by the 'next generation' every 10 years.

o   The success with which the CPC gradually loosens its grip and opens up to legal and political reform or lose its mandate.

Continuing ability of Party to retain loyalty of the citizens

According to <u>Martin Ivens, political correspondent, London's Sunday Times</u>: *"Twenty years ago, after the Tiananmen Square 'incident', the Communist Party imposed an awesomely successful settlement on its subject population: you will have economic freedoms and capitalist-style growth provided you don't challenge our monopoly of political power."*

That 'settlement' has been in force for 20 years, bolstered by continuing export-led economic growth at around 10% pa, lifting 100s of millions out of dire poverty. Starting with the so-called banking crisis of 2008, export no longer looks to be a certainty. The Party has acknowledged that and in his recent address to the 90th anniversary of the CPC, President Hu lists domestic consumption as one of the new thrusts for the next five-year plan.

That is all very well if inflation has not raised its ugly head.

With affluence comes its twin brother, increased consumption. But the world, according to some experts, is reaching its natural capacity to provide adequate food for the population, slated to grow from today's <u>nearly 7 billion to 9 billion in 2050</u>. If they are correct, then food price inflation is inevitable. Never mind shortage of water. Incidentally, there are global knock-on effects of Chinese inflation.

Debt cities are piling up to improve infrastructure

The number of airports, metros, business and residential estates being developed is mind boggling and so is <u>the debt</u> - estimated at $2.2 trillion often through special investment instruments such as Local Government Finance Vehicles (LGFV) off the cities' books - usually backed by inflated land valuation. So, on the one hand there is a surplus of $3 trillion, but on the other hand there is a huge national debt. If any unexpected event triggers foreclosure on some of these major project loans.... Additionally, from data available, it would appear that loans to state corporations are cheaper and easier to get than that available to private firms.

During 2012, Foxconn maker of iPhones and other mobile gadgets announced it will be increasing its use of industrial robots from today's 10,000 to 1 million in three years. This is partly to offset labor costs which have doubled due to industrial relations issues including suicides by factory workers. At present it employs over 1 million workers in China. It has not revealed how many of these will be let go. What is clear is that its performance from $35m profit to $280 million loss is largely due to labor costs. If this replacement of labor by robots is not a one-off case. Trouble lies ahead for China.

In conclusion, without continuing improvement in living standards, the 'settlement' will fall apart. It is finely-balanced unstable equilibrium.

Wealth inequality and corruption

Another of President's Hu's 90th Anniversary address warns about corruption. This is amazing as most other countries try to sweep the issue under the carpet. So the issue must be serious enough. Interestingly, in June, 2011, the People's Bank of China inadvertently released a confidential report online. It mentions 10,000 corrupt officials who escaped with £80 billion over 15 years. One assumes that if this is the published figure, the real figure must be much larger. Despite regular arrests, convictions and sometimes executions, of some of very senior officials corruption continues apace. New websites that expose corruption have started, many crashing due to overload of traffic.

The worst part about corruption is not only that money is siphoned off into private pockets but often the results are devastating in terms of health and food safety, such as melamine-tainted baby milk, or medicines that contain no active ingredients, or meat fed with chemicals (clenbuterol) that help to reduce fat to produce lean meat but could cause human heart palpitations, shoddy public buildings - such as possibly schools that collapsed in the Sichuan earthquake in 2008, never fully investigated, and highways or railways.

On July 23, 2011, a high-speed train was halted purportedly by lightening at Wenzhou on the Beijing-Shanghai line. A second high speed train ploughed into it, allegedly because of traffic signal failures.

Government's initial reaction was two-fold, to physically remove evidence of the train wreck and to order the media not to report adverse information. The power of the Internet and the rage of the citizens, both directly affected and at large put paid to the latter. Thousands of citizens descended on the site with flowers and other tokens of sympathy. Demands for an open and honest investigation have been acknowledged by the government. Even the official paper People's Daily joined in with an editorial that said that although China needed such modern developments it did not need 'blood smeared GDP'. Premier Hu visited the site and paid his respects. He also promised that anyone found to be guilty will be punished. Railway Minister Liu Zhijun had already been suspended in February along with some other senior officials. More heads are likely to roll. Not least because, in addition to this accident, there have been many incidents of faults along the network due to its accelerated development and opening to coincide with the 90th Anniversary.

Following the rail accident, news is emerging that several <u>bridges</u> built in the last 10-20 years seem to be suffering from early decay. It now transpires that the prime contractor who won the tender, not always in open competition, would then pass the work down to a lesser company, sometimes several levels below, each level with bribery, so that by the level the work actually took place, the funds were not sufficient for quality materials or work. Perhaps China needs an Anna Hazare.

Unless corruption is brought to brook, the credibility of the Party itself is at stake.

A second aspect of the have's and have not's is the disparity between urban dwellers and migrant workers from the countryside. It is not well known that migrant workers (est at 150m) <u>do not have the rights</u> of urban residents. In some ways they are just tolerated. There is growing frustration and also growing awareness by government that this state of affairs cannot carry on much longer without <u>major unrest</u> amongst mainly young males living in dormitories with basic amenities. Steps are being taken to recognize migrant workers as 'business as usual' and not a temporary glitch.

Another aspect is that of <u>land seizures</u> where farmers and small holders have their land seized, often well below market value in the cause of factories, infrastructure projects or urban development. This has given rise to increased petitions. But that is seen by many as a waste of time. Those with Internet access, which is growing phenomenally, online complaints and exchanges of frustration is on the increase.

Unless government can deal with these issues effectively - and we do not mean by suppressing online interactions - things will boil over from electronic to flesh and blood, sooner rather than later. China is discovering that a sophisticated knowledge economy and authoritarian one-party rule may not be entirely compatible.

There is also a marked increase in reported incidents involving the public and the police, often the Chengguan - urban security guards. Minor riots have been reported in various town and provinces. So far these have been isolated incidents. Government, of course, worries that these could somehow coalesce into something that could threaten its power. Most analysts think this is unlikely. But there will come a 'tipping point' when all of a sudden the much feared 'jasmine revolution' actual occurs. Microbloggers increased in 2011 four-fold from 63m to over 500m on Sina Weibo, the equivalent of Twitter. It is increasingly difficult for the authorities to censor peer-to-peer interactions and for individuals to broadcast their views. In 2011, users were required to register in their real names rather than use pseudonyms. This is probably to enable the authorities to track who is saying what.

But to quote Mao: it takes *"one spark to start a prairie fire."* And, technology is on the side of the people, despite efforts by government to control and censor.

Central government sway over Tibet and Xinjiang

We have dwelt on this topic at length and will not repeat ourselves here, except to say that unless China solves the minorities dilemma, the periphery could trigger unrest elsewhere. In May, 2011, the death of an Inner Mongolian herder run over by a coal truck caused the largest protest since 1991. Fortunately, the protesters were against miners and police rather than between Mongolians and Han Chinese. After prolonged unrest, the driver was eventually arrested, convicted and sentenced to death.

One trigger point will be when the current Dalai Lama passes away. China will try to impose upon the Tibetans his successor. The religious hierarchy will try to identify his reincarnation as they have done for centuries. The current impasse will turn into a new major power struggle. But who can tell what the outcome will be.

Smooth transition of senior leaders every 10 years

China is probably unique in that as an autocratic state the transition of power has been smooth and bloodless (at least since 1996). Patrick Chovanec a professor at Tsinghua University's School of Economics and Management in Beijing, China has written an excellent paper in May 2011 on the governance of China: *Everything You Need to Know about China's Leadership Transition*

Every five years, the President and Prime Minster are re-confirmed or step down; after the second term and new leaders are chosen. Retirement at 68 is mandatory. So in November 2012, apart from the President designate, Xi Jinping and the Premier designate, Li Keqiang, all other seven members of Central Politburo Standing Committee (PSC) retired. They were replaced by five (to complete a smaller PSC) all due to retire in five years.

If all goes according to plan, China will continue on its trajectory to become the second most economically powerful nation well before 2038. There are some signs that there is some tension amongst the leadership. Premier Wen since August 2010 has been speaking up on political reform. Others are attempting to re-assess the Party's response to the so-called Tiananmen incident. According to Dr Kissinger in his book *On China*, he says that he met younger people who are reassessing the Great Cultural Revolution as something not entirely an unmitigated disaster, but with some benefits such as cutting through bureaucratic stagnation, or uniting people through a sense of common purpose - which he hastens to add, he does not share. There is talk of 'universal values' such as freedom and democracy. Archival material has recently been released that enabled Frank Dikötter to write *Mao's Great Famine*.

However, there seems to be some backlash. Revival of Maoist art and song and the removal of a statue of Kong Fuzi in front of the newly re-opened National Museum points to an indication of some kind of doctrinal if not power struggle. But the predicted handover to Xi and Li seems to indicate the 'moderates' have won – for now.

Will the CPC make legal and political reform or lose its mandate

So far, the CPC has not been good at human rights. Ai Weiwei is one example. Another high-profile example is Liu Xiabo who was awarded the Nobel Peace Prize in 2010, but was not permitted to travel to Oslo to collect it. In June 2011, there were reports of a blind lawyer, <u>Chen Guangcheng</u> beaten and his home vandalised because of his activism exposing a local government programme of forced abortions. Though he was eventually allowed to migrate to the US after escaping from house arrest. There are <u>many others</u> according to Amnesty International. One thing the Party has learnt not to execute dissidents. That would only make them martyrs as Chiang Kaishek's KMT did when they executed Chinese communists in the early 1900s.

As China progresses from a 'developing' nation into a middle-income one by 2020, the leaders will need to face up to instituting legal and political reform, where the judiciary is independent and the state is autonomous from the Party. At present, as Prof Chovanac says in his paper (above) the three are slightly different aspects of each other with the Party on top and the judiciary at the bottom. The longer major reforms are postponed, the stronger the head of steam for change will build up. This time, if the population revolts, it will not be looking to the Tiananmen Square incident for inspiration but rather to Tahir Square, Tunisia and Libya. Without major reforms, the CPC's mandate may come to an abrupt end before 2038.

Paradoxically, at another level China is loosening its reins, such as not only tolerating but encouraging contact with the West, not only through goods and luxury items but through culture. For instance, since 2000, many <u>multi-day rock concerts</u> have been allowed or, in some cases, sponsored by the local Communist Party. These music festivals have been held not only in the expected affluent and westernised coastal regions but as far afield as the grasslands of Inner Mongolia and highlands of Yunnan. This loosening up has the tendency of encouraging the young to look out beyond the boundaries of China. Once they start to glimpse the freedom available to young people elsewhere in music, art, and literature, they soon start to ask questions about freedom in other more important spheres like democracy and human rights.

6.5 Indian challenges?

India, by contrast, is relatively stable. However there are some serious challenges that could render India unstable. The challenges we envisage are:

o   The continuing ability of the Indian National Congress Party to either hold its majority or to be able to govern with a workable coalition.

o   The patience of Indian 'have nots', especially the militant dissidents in tolerating the rich and government officials in their 'unfair' share of wealth, often through corruption.

o   The ability of the Indian central government to continue to hold the country together, against the desire of some states to declare UDI.

o   The shaky relationship of India with Pakistan, especially over Kashmir, leading to an indigenous Indian Muslim insurgency.

o   The success with which genuine democracy becomes accepted practice in India.

Will Indian National Congress Party continue to govern

Although the Indian National Congress Party has been in power for most of the 60 years since Independence, it seldom enjoyed an absolute majority. Fortunately, there are many more parties than in the US or UK, so Congress ends up being on top. But with increasing literacy and a growing middle class, the status quo may not remain.

Wealth inequality and corruption

In her book, *Broken Republic*, Arundhati Roy, warns against the rising anger amongst tribal groups amongst whom live the Maoists. In theory, the positive discrimination that India has practiced since Independence has helped the Dalits to a large extent, but has not been of much use to the tribal population as the legislation is more about removing barriers than about providing support either financial or material. Now with growing demand for minerals, Indian mining firms and the government are finding both tribals and Maoists in their way. The same conflict applies when new dams are proposed for either irrigation or power purposes. There is no happy scenario ahead.

   The problem with corruption in India is that it is pervasive. It does not only affect major contracts - common to many developing nations, but down to everyday transactions such as obtaining a marriage license or a tax refund. The latest attempt to curb corruption is proposed legislation to make only accepting or soliciting bribes illegal. That gives the briber some incentive to report incidents, whereas at present both the giver and taker are subject to criminal action, deterring anyone from reporting bribery.

On August 16, 2011, protesters in several major cities clashed with police over the arrest of the leader of the biggest anti-corruption movement - Anna Hazare. Many commentators in the leading papers sided with Mr Hazare, one even declaring that the PM Manmohan Singh had disgraced himself by allowing this to happen. Curiously, Arundhati Roy (see above para) has taken a contrary view and sees setting up a corruption ombudsman as adding to the problem rather than solving it, on the basis that it will be yet another non-democratic institution. Nevertheless on August 29, government agreed to Shri Hazare's demands and will initiate legislation that will include an Ombudsman, covering all levels of government, both civil servants and MPs at both federal and regional levels, and have a means for citizens to air their grievances without retribution.

Will Indian central government hold country together

Some eight new states were split from existing states after Independence. There are other ethnic groups still fighting for autonomy, such as Gorkhaland in northern West Bengal. Each split was justified on a case-by-case basis. But the more splits that are approved, the more other minorities clamor for autonomy. The worst case are the four recently-created border states seceded from Assam in the north east, including Arunachal Pradesh which is partly occupied by China since the 1962 border conflict.

The tension between some states, especially those on the borders as well as those where the Naxalite Marxists hold sway poses a serious problem to the central government.

Will India and Pakistan continue to co-exist

Enough has been said and written about India, Pakistan and Kashmir. The worrying factor that has raised its ugly head is the emergence of an indigenous Indian Mujahedeen that is suspected of the July 2011 Mumbai bombings though not proven.

Will genuine democracy become accepted practice

There are at least two India's: one that sits with its peers in the UN, Commonwealth of Nations, ASEAN and other international august bodies; the other very local and traditional and pseudo-feudal. Most villages and villagers, especially in the north of India, pay lip service to national and state laws. They practice, instead, age-old law of the village council, *khap panchayat*. Unelected village elders, often belonging to families of landlords and money-lenders dictate on matters as dispirit as marriages and land disputes. Khap leaders contend they provide cohesion and stability. Central government sees them as <u>holding back modernity and progress</u>. So-called honor killings for marriages or elopements that have not been approved are a case in point. And these often are caused by breaking of traditional caste rules, which themselves have been outlawed since 1947. Some khap panchayats have tried to ban women from having mobile phones as they see it is one way to be independent of the men-folk.

Note: khap panchayats are self-established entities that seek to reinforce caste practices and are not to be confused with *gram panchayats*, set up by edict after Independence to foster village self-rule, a sub-division of district which is a sub-division of state. Sort of like the British parish council.

Earlier, we pointed out that voting in many villages is often unanimous, directly by the elders. This partly because of the power of the elders and also because of low literacy which causes the farmers to look to the elders for direction. This phenomenon is separate from the issues of khap panchayat. Such is not real democracy.

The growing middle class is now awakening to the fact that politicians use them and the urban wealth for resources but count on the villagers for power. So far this has led to grumbling in tea shops. But sometime in the foreseeable future, the patience will break and politics will not be the same again in India.

6.6 How well will China and India innovate?

Just as a few decades ago, there was a perception that the Japanese could only copy and improve but not innovate, this perception today applies to China and India. Then, Japan countered by setting up MITI, the Ministry of International Trade and Technology, that fostered investments in technology which, together with private investment, enabled it to catch up with and in many industries to surpass the West. In the 60 years since the end of WWII, Japan is second only to the US in number of patents filed.

China and India realize that to succeed in the 21st Century, copying and improving is not good enough. They will need to innovate by investing in scientific research and higher education. Both have set up first class universities focused on technology. Both run national five-year plans and technology and innovation loom large in those plans.

Chinese innovation

According to McKinsey, China's next five-year plan (2012-2017) aims to transform the world's second-largest economy from an investment-driven dynamo into a global powerhouse with a steadier and more stable trajectory. The plan affects domestic and foreign companies in all industries. To help senior managers decode and understand its provisions, McKinsey analyzed the potential impact on 33 industries. Two dimensions stood out: the effect on their profit pools and competitive landscapes.

"The plan characterizes a handful of industries as emerging battlegrounds where countries will be competing for technological leadership during the next wave of development. These industries, including new energy sources and biotechnology, are distinguished by their high profit growth potential and moderate state oversight. In these areas, the government has dedicated itself to incubating national and global champions by helping them gain leading technologies and expanding their commercial capabilities.

"China's ambitious 12th five-year plan builds on decades of unprecedented economic growth. It seeks to transform the economy from an investment-led powerhouse focused exclusively on GDP growth to a sustainable model that balances growth with social harmony, and innovation with environmental protection. Whether or not the full slate of aspirations can be achieved, the direction in which China's leaders hope to move the country is clear."

In the meantime, China is forging ahead with *patenting inventions*, a strong indicator of innovative capabilities. The World Intellectual Property Organization predicted that either in 2012, China will overtake Germany as number 3 in terms of *international* patents filed at around 20,000 applications, still behind Japan at 35,000 and the US at around

45,000. India is somewhat behind at well under 2,000. If one looks at *national* patent applications, namely the stage before an organization applies for an international application, the picture is even starker: US at 450,000, China and Japan both around 350,000, with Korea, Germany and EU collectively between 100,000 and 150,000.

At a less formal level, the number of published scientific papers is another indicator of innovation. In 2011, China will be the second largest source (after the US), having beaten Britain in 2008. It should be noted, however, that there is widespread concern regarding academic and scientific fraud in China. If this practice is not reduced at least if not eliminated, it could stymie China's thrust in innovation.

In late 2010, Tianhe-1A briefly became the world's fastest supercomputer. Then in October 2011, the Sunway Bluelight MPP broke the petaflop barrier (a quadrillion floating point operations per second). It is amongst the world's top 20 computers. Not only did it use Chinese chips but it also achieved a low power consumption compared to its peers.

China is now no 2 in venture capital investments at $7.6bn pa. Nearly 800 firms (many based in Silicon Valley) have invested in over 2,000 Chinese firms.

In 2011, China was midway into setting up an alternative for the US GPS. It is already operational over China and surrounds, but will cover the globe by 2020. This is in defence of any future curtailment of GPS by a future xenophobic government. It will also allow the Chinese military to use satellites to pinpoint targets and weapon systems much as the US GPS does. And it is pursuing a space exploration programme that in a decade or so will put a Chinese person on the moon. Chinese solar energy industry has overtaken Germany, even in terms of new installations in Germany. This is partly due to price advantage, but also Germany as also some others have removed subsidies for local solar firms.

At a practical level, China is number one in solar energy, it has invented several electric cars, with billions being spent on electric car charging station infrastructure. It is active with wind turbines, wave energy transformers, and - of course - biotechnology.

Additionally, China is encouraging its nuclear scientists in their search for the 'holy grail' of nuclear energy, 'cold' *nuclear fusion*. Current technology is based on nuclear fission where uranium molecules break-up and give up their energy as they transform into lower energy plutonium - with all the negative consequences of waste nuclear material and the need to contain the reaction and protect the plant from earthquakes, tsunamis and so forth. Nuclear fusion, by contrast, is where deuterium, an isotope of hydrogen extracted from sea water, known as *'heavy hydrogen'* is fused with tritium, another rare radioactive isotope of hydrogen releasing enormous energy - all at non-threatening temperatures. It is estimated that one litre of sea water could produce the same amount of energy as 300 litres of petrol.

As a footnote, don't forget China invented a viable electric cycle that over a few years has reached $11bn worldwide. Admittedly, some of it is in place of ordinary bikes, but many more are substitutes for cars, reducing pollution.

Indian innovation

India, as in many other areas, is lagging behind in innovation. The number of science and engineering graduates, the number of published scientific papers and the number of patents files all lag behind. This is partly historical and partly due to lack of heavy government financial and other support.

Nevertheless, in many areas Indian innovation is ahead of China's: in software, pharmaceuticals, and in mobile digital technology. McKinsey predicts that India's internet users will increase five-fold by 2015 to 35% of the population and three quarters will choose mobile access. A local Android based smartphone costs less than half that of iPhone. Applications, both 'smart' and traditional abound for both urban and rural users, the latter helping to improve both productivity and get better prices for their produce. With 830m subscribers of mobile phones, second only to China and an average of 10m devices pm, mobile technology is the technology of choice for Indians. With long battery life, local phones are outselling global branded ones. Furthermore, they are beginning to penetrate overseas markets such as in Bangladesh, Sri Lanka and Africa.

Although huge investments have been earmarked for improved infrastructure, so far the actual spending has been lower than that planned. This is proving to be a major obstacle to economic and, to a degree, social improvement. But plans are afoot to accelerate this investment: in roads, in electricity and other infrastructure.

Mobile and other telecoms technology is being innovated by India - low cost handsets and services for poor and rural communities are being developed.

The most telling sign that India is moving from a 'developing' nation status to that of a 'developed' nation is the number of overseas returnees. Many of these are graduates of the prestigious world-class IITs and IIMs. They bring back with them experience gained with world-class innovative firms. That combined with the emergence of a vibrant and growing middle class and domestic market may well prove to be a tipping point for India.

Also, don't forget the Tata Nano. It is not a radical invention. Yet, it created a 1 lakh rupee (around $2,000) car that existing manufacturers thought not feasible. That is innovation!

In conclusion

Although both China and India at present lag behind the US, Japan, Germany and South Korea in actual innovative products, their accelerating program of innovation means that, together with catching up on GDP, their future products are likely to catch up with leading countries. In other words, together with GDP based on population, innovation will make China and India preeminent in the latter part of the 21st Century - as they were up to the 18th Century.

IN CLOSING

As we said in our introduction China and India may be a case of *Hidden Dragon, Crouching Tiger*. Interestingly, India is often portrayed as a tiger or elephant – both endangered species. But as we hope this book will have indicated India is on a growth path, not in decline – despite what Ramachandra Guha has to say.

China is often portrayed as a dragon. That begs the question: is it a Chinese or a Western dragon? A Western dragon is usually deemed a *'bad guy'* ready for the chop by St George. A Chinese dragon, by contrast, is a *'good guy'* bringing rain and enabling the annual harvest; and a symbol of the imperial mandate from heaven.

As Napoleon once said about China: *"Let the dragon sleep. For when she wakes, the world will tremble."* Well, after slumbering for nearly 200 years, China has awakened and the world is indeed prepared to tremble. But, given the right following wind, perhaps there is no need to. Our view is that neither country, by natural inclination, is prone to aggression and imperialism in the mould of European colonialism. So, despite any saber rattling, perhaps the territorial conflict in the China Seas will sort themselves out in the near future. And the on-going border demarcation dispute between China and India will also be resolved without military intervention.

At the beginning of the 19th century China and India were the countries with the highest GDP. Sometime soon during the 21st centuries, they will be so again. In centuries to come, perhaps historian will see the 19th and 20th centuries as aberrations when for a brief span of time European (and its offshoot, American) economies reigned.

AFTERWORD: EIGHT WAYS CHINA IS CHANGING YOUR WORLD

We largely agree with the author of the following which has been extracted from:

BBC News – http://www.bbc.co.uk/news/world-asia-19797989
By Angus Foster
BBC News, Beijing
October 15, 2012

China's ruling Communist Party meets from November 8, 2012 to rubber-stamp sweeping changes that will put in place the country's leaders for the next 10 years.

Here are eight reasons - eight being an auspicious number in China - why the world should pay attention to what happens in the secretive corridors of Beijing's Great Hall of the People.

'To get rich is glorious'

It is now 35 years since former leader Deng Xiaoping's catchy slogan signaled China's opening to the world and ushered in one of the biggest economic success stories in human history.

Its economy has gone from being rather smaller than Italy's to the world's second largest, and is now home to one million US$ millionaires. By the time the new generation of leaders hands over power to the next in 2022/23, China could be challenging the US for top spot.

This transformation has changed the way the world does business. Cheap Chinese labor has helped dampen prices in the West for everything from moccasins to mops to mobile phones. It is now the biggest investor in Africa, promising to shift the continent's focus away from Europe and the US for the first time in two centuries. And China is now the biggest foreign holder of US government debt - a threatening stick, or a foolhardy bet?

The key question now is whether the new leaders can keep the economy growing at the same rate as in the past, and help the rest of the world recover. Most Western analysts expect it to slow from 10% a year to a still impressive 6-7%, but argue that deep reforms are needed if China is to become a rich rather than middle-income country.

Growth should help create the world's biggest middle class, eager to enjoy creature comforts like cars and air conditioning, whatever the environmental cost.

Every feast must have its end

China has been growing so fast it has scarcely stopped to consider the environmental cost.

The results are sobering. Rapid industrialization and a building boom saw China overtake the US as the world's biggest emitter of greenhouse gases in 2007. Seven of the world's most polluted cities are in China. Each year it causes 500,000 to 750,000 premature deaths.

The damage is not just inside China. Airborne pollution including mercury and lead is carried across borders into neighboring countries, and across the Pacific where it falls on the US West Coast.

China's leaders do now appear determined to clean up the worst excesses, but the scale of the task is daunting.

"If you look at the size of the economy and its population, these two factors alone show how complex it's going to be," says Edgar Cua of the Asian Development Bank.

It means China will be central to any future agreements on climate change. It has refused to limit its greenhouse gas emissions, preferring to cut 'carbon intensity' - the carbon released per unit of economic output - by 40-45% by 2020. But with the economy growing so fast, and China relying on coal for up to 70% of its energy needs, greenhouse gas emissions will still rise by 60% from their present level, even if the carbon intensity target is met.

Teach the kids Mandarin?

China has long fascinated the West, but its emergence as an economic power has seen a new burgeoning of interest in its culture and language.

Thirty years ago, only its inscrutable leaders were recognized in the West. Now people like actress Zhang Ziyi, basketball player Yao Ming and artist Zhang Xiaogang are global figures.

Meanwhile schools across Europe and the US are offering Mandarin classes to children as young as six, and during the Olympics, Chinese script could be seen on adverts on some London buses.

China's government has sought to capture the zeitgeist, helping set up several hundred Confucius Institutes around the world whose overt goal is teaching Chinese, but which also project soft power.

The number of Mandarin speakers is set to grow strongly, especially in Asia, but is it really able to challenge English as a global language? Not any time soon, most experts argue, pointing to its infuriating tones and a script which takes years to master.

Keep the peace

China adopted the phrase 'peaceful rise' to try and assure nervous neighbors that its new-found economic clout would not turn it into a bully.

But territorial disputes with Japan, the Philippines and Vietnam - and simmering tensions with the US - sometimes give the words a hollow ring.

China's People's Liberation Army is the world's largest, at three million strong, and its official budget is rising fast. Its first aircraft carrier has just gone into service and it is believed to be investing heavily in stealth technology, space warfare and cyber security.

These are natural developments for a country of its size and influence, China argues, and do not signal it has changed tack.

"Every country has to defend its security and territorial interests, but it doesn't mean we have to become aggressive, that way you can alienate even your friends," said Wu Jianmin, former ambassador to France.

But the real question is how China's new leaders pitch policy towards the US. They are younger and have more experience of the outside world, so can they set aside the entrenched suspicions among their rival militaries? History suggests the inevitable frictions between a superpower and its upstart challenger will lead to more tensions than detente.

Next person on the moon to be Chinese?

China's Communist Party paints the century before it came to power in 1949 as one of humiliation by the West. So China's successful space program is lauded as proof their country has regained its international standing.

But the huge cost is controversial given that 150m Chinese still live on $1 a day or less.

Having already sent an unmanned craft to orbit the moon, China has said it will send its first probe to land there in 2013. It has also spoken of preliminary plans to put humans on the moon, though no date has been set.

If the mission goes ahead, TV pictures beamed into the world's living rooms will also be flagging up China's challenge to the world's predominant space power, the US.

The end for elephants, rhinos, manta rays, pigs...

Newly-wealthy Chinese are blamed for fuelling the poaching of endangered species for use as aphrodisiacs, ornaments or to put in their soup.

Thousands of African elephants are killed each year for their ivory, which Chinese carvers prize, and China's government has been criticized for not properly policing its ivory trade.

The problem is that economic reforms which have lifted hundreds of millions of people out of poverty have also created voracious consumers.

Pork consumption gives a good idea of the impact. China now consumes five times more pork than in 1979, and is now home to 460m pigs, half the world's total.

But feeding them is impossible given the shortage of land. So farmers have resorted to importing up to 60% of the world's soyabean exports, pushing up prices for everyone else, and raising real fears over the industry's environmental impact.

In future, the pressures are likely to intensify as China seeks to feed 21% of the world's population with only 9% of its cultivated land. Some experts believe we will all have to get used to higher food prices, and to Chinese farmers buying up more and more overseas land.

Better to travel than read 10,000 books

As recently as 1995, applying for a passport to leave China was a six-month endurance test of bureaucracy, and most applicants were officials.

Now it can be done in a few days, and millions of Chinese are taking advantage of their government's new openness to travel overseas as tourists or students.

China's tourists are now the world's third biggest spenders, behind those from Germany and the US, and 70m Chinese travelled overseas in 2011, compared to 4.5m in 1995. Most stay close to home, in places like Hong Kong, Macau and Thailand. But increasing numbers are heading for the US or France, as well as less obvious destinations like Trier, the birthplace of Karl Marx. On Paris' Bateaux Mouches river cruises, as the sights are picked out in one language after another, Mandarin now comes ahead of Japanese.

Each year about 300,000 Chinese students are also heading abroad, especially to universities in the US and Australia. They want the kudos of a foreign education to get a better job when they return home. Some also see it as a way to dodge the exhausting entry test for China's own universities.

Buying up the planet

The wealth that has been created inside China has surged around the world.

Chinese demand has caused spikes in prices for commodities like copper - needed to cable up rapidly growing cities and infrastructure. It has reinvigorated Europe's luxury goods makers like Louis Vuitton and Hermes, whose products are de rigueur in China's status-obsessed and gift-giving culture. And it is transforming prestige wine sales - China now buys more Bordeaux than Germany.

Perhaps the most spectacular impact, some would call it a bubble, is on Chinese art. Three of the 10 most expensive paintings sold in 2011 were by Chinese artists, including the most expensive, a $57.2m work by

Qi Baishi.

The next phase is likely to see China's industrial giants starting to look overseas for new markets and new expertise.

That will be controversial because most of them are controlled by the Communist Party. In areas like telecommunications and energy, they could threaten trade rows with the West.

SOURCES

In producing this book we consulted (or at least dipped into) the following - amongst other material:

Reports:

- A CEO's guide to innovation in China - February 2012, McKinsey Quarterly
- China and Britain in a Changing World - November 2007 , Mme Fu Ying, Chinese Ambassador to Great Britain (to 2009), at the RSA, London
- China & India: What you need to know - August 22-29, 2005, Business Week
- China - 2020: Key policy outcomes of the 17th Party Congress - November 2007, Nottingham University, China Policy Institute
- China Rising: special issue - November 10, 2007, New Scientist
- Facts and Myths in the Globalization Debate – Vivek Wadhwa, Duke University, 2008
- Reflections on doing business in China, November 2006, Institute of Directors (UK)
- Scenarios for India & China 2015: Implications for the City of London - October 2006, SAMI Consulting and Oxford Analytica
- Sold on India, Nov 25, 2005, Business Week
- The Trouble with India – March 15, 2007, Business Week
- The Tiger in Front: A survey of India and China – March 5, 2005, The Economist
- The World in 2036 – The Economist

Books:

- Analects - Confucius (Kongzi), thinker and social philosopher
- Billions of Entrepreneurs: How China and India Are Reshaping Their Futures and Yours - Tarun Khanna, Professor, Harvard Business School
- China, Inc., How the Next Superpower Challenges America and the World – Ted C Fishman, writer
- The China Price: True Cost of Chinese Competitive Advantage - Alexandra Harney, head of research at management consultancy
- China Road: A Journey into the Future of a Rising Power - Rob Gifford, journalist
- China: A Wolf in the World? - George Walden, former British diplomat to China during Cultural Revolution
- Chindia: How China and India Are Revolutionizing Global Business - edited by Peter Engardio, Business Week
- Chindia Rising: How China and India Will Benefit Your Business - Jagdish N Sheth, Professor, Emory University
- The Chinese Century: The Rising Chinese Economy and Its Impact on the Global Economy, the Balance of Power, and Your Job – Oded Shenkar, Ohio State University
- The Discovery of India - Jawaharlal Nehru, first Premier of India
- The Dragon's Gift: The real story of China in Africa - Deborah Brautigam, academic specializing on Africa and China
- The Dragon and the Elephant: China, India and the New World Order - David Smith, Economics Editor, Sunday Times
- Dr Ambedkar And Untouchability: Analysing And Fighting Caste - Christophe Jaffrelot
- For All the Tea in China: Espionage, Empire and the secret formula for the world's favourite drink Sarah Rose
- The Genius of China: 3,000 Years of Science, Discovery and Invention - Robert Temple (based on work by Joseph Needham)
- Getting China and India Right: Strategies for Leveraging the World's Fastest Growing Economies for Global Advantage - Anil K. Gupta, Business School, University of Maryland and Haiyan Wang, Managing Partner, China India Institute
- Growling Tiger, Roaring Dragon: India, China, and the New World Order - David Smith, Economics Editor, Sunday Times
- The Hindu View of Life - Dr Sarvepalli Radhakrishnan, philosopher and first Indian Vice President and second President

- How the West was Lost - Dambisa Moyo, formerly Goldman Sachs
- I Ching Book of Changes (the Chinese oracle) - attributed to Emperor Fu Hsi
- India: A Portrait - Patrick French, British writer and historian
- India's Century: The Age of Entrepreneurship in the World's Biggest Democracy - Kamal Nath, India's Commerce & Industry Minister
- India's Unending Journey - Finding Balance in a Time of Change - Sir Mark Tully, broadcaster
- In Spite of the Gods - the Strange Rise of Modern India - Edward Luce, journalist, Financial Times
- Losing Control: The Emerging Threats to Western Prosperity - Stephen D. King, HSBC chief economist
- The Mahabharata
- Making Sense of Chindia - Jairam Ramesh, senior Indian politician
- Mao's Great Famine - Frank Dikötter, Professor, University of London
- Mao's Last Revolution - Roderick MacFarquhar, Michael Schoenhals, academics: Harvard and Lund, resp.
- On China - Henry Kissinger, retired diplomat and statesman
- Opium Wars – Julia Lovell, historian
- The Party: The Secret World of China's Communist Rulers - Richard McGregor, journalist, Financial Times
- The Ramayana
- Rivals: How the Power Struggle Between China, India, and Japan Will Shape Our Next Decade - Bill Emmott, former editor of The Economist
- The Scramble for China: Foreign Devils in the Qing Empire, 1832-1914 - Robert Bickers, history professor, Bristol University
- The Story of India - Michael Wood, BBC (book based on TV series)
- Superpower? The Amazing Race between China's Hare and India's Tortoise - Raghav Bahl, the founder, controlling shareholder, and managing director of Network 18, India's largest television news and business network.
- Tao Te Ching - attributed to Lao Tzu (Laozi), philosopher
- Ten Thousand Miles Without a Cloud - Sun Shuyun, traveler, writer
- An Introduction to Transcendental Meditation - Robert Roth, meditator
- The True Story of Ah Q - Lu Xun, author

- Views from an Indian Bus – Alistair Shearer, cultural historian ISBN 978-1-909424-13-5
- When a Billion Chinese Jump: How China will save Mankind - or destroy it - Jonathan Watts, journalist, the Guardian
- When China Rules the World: The Rise of the Middle Kingdom and the End of the Western World - Martin Jacques, journalist, the Guardian
- Why the West Rules - for Now - Ian Morris, historian, Stanford University
- With the Empress Dowager - Katherine Carl, painter and author
- The World Is Flat: A Brief History of the Twenty-first Century – Thomas L Friedman, journalist, New York Times
- The Writing on the Wall: China and the West in the 21st Century - Will Hutton, Journalist and The Work Foundation
- 'Zero-Sum World' - Gideon Rachman, FT's chief foreign correspondent

Specific websites referenced in the book:
Chapter 1
- Chindia - http://en.wikipedia.org/wiki/Chindia
- East India Company - http://www.sscnet.ucla.edu/southasia/History/British/EAco.html
- Duke of Wellington - http://www.infobritain.co.uk/Duke_Of_Wellington.htm
- GDP data - http://en.wikipedia.org/wiki/List_of_countries_by_GDP_%28nominal%29

Chapter 2
- Old Summer Palace - http://www.travelchinaguide.com/attraction/beijing/yuanmingyuan.htm
- Story of Ah Q - http://history.cultural-china.com/en/60H7252H12435.html
- Dr M Singh's Oxford honorary degree acceptance speech - http://www.hindu.com/thehindu/nic/0046/pmspeech.htm

Section 2.1

- Five Classics - http://history.cultural-china.com/en/173History4610.html
- First Emperor - http://www.sacu.org/qinemperor.html
- 60-year calendar cycle - http://www.webexhibits.org/calendars/calendar-chinese.html
- Yellow Emperor - http://history.cultural-china.com/en/46History1159.html
- Genius of China - http://www.curledup.com/geniusch.htm

Section 2.2

- British Raj - http://www.bbc.co.uk/history/british/modern/independence1947_01.shtml
- Ramayana - http://ramayana4.tripod.com/summ.htm
- Mahabharata - http://larryavisbrown.homestead.com/files/xeno.mahabsynop.htm
- Aryans - http://www.indhistory.com/aryan.html
- Sanskrit - http://www.hinduwebsite.com/general/sanskrit.asp
- Maurya Dynasty - http://www.livius.org/man-md/mauryas/mauryas.html
- Gupta Dynasty - http://www.iloveindia.com/history/ancient-india/gupta-dynasty.html
- Akbar the Great - http://www.boloji.com/index.cfm?md=Content&sd=Articles&ArticleID=793
- Ancient Indian inventions and discoveries - http://www.thisismyindia.com/ancient_india/achievement-of-ancient-india.html
- The Vedas - http://www.bbc.co.uk/religion/religions/hinduism/texts/texts.shtml

Section 2.3 & 2.5

- China's 20th Century timeline - http://www.beijingmadeeasy.com/beijing-history/20th-century-chinese-history-timeline

Section 2.4 & 2.6

- India's 20th Century timeline -
  http://www.kamat.com/database/content/20th_century/

Section 3.1

- Facts & myths in globalization debate -
  http://openinnovation.berkeley.edu/speaker_series/Wadhwa_11_23_09.pdf
- Chinese women successes -
  http://www.thesundaytimes.co.uk/sto/Magazine/Features/article625318.ece

Section 3.2

- IIT success stories -
  http://www.businessweek.com/1998/49/b3607011.htm
- Facts & myths in globalization debate -
  http://openinnovation.berkeley.edu/speaker_series/Wadhwa_11_23_09.pdf
- Indian women successes - http://sudarshan-ema.blogspot.co.uk/2010/01/nyt-report-on-women-ceos-in-india-basis.html

Section 3.3

- Chinese names - http://blog.myheritage.com/2008/10/the-structure-of-chinese-surna/

Section 3.4

- India's diversity -
  http://www.preservearticles.com/201105257074/short-essay-on-diversity-in-indian-culture.html
- Caste among non-Hindus - http://www.examrace.com/Study-Material/Sociology/Caste-system-among-nonHindus.html

Section 3.5

- Ten thousand Miles without a Cloud -
  http://www.guardian.co.uk/books/2003/aug/02/featuresreviews.guardianreview4

Section 3.6

- Four Books - http://history.cultural-china.com/en/173History4610.html

Section 3.7

- Kumbh Mela - http://www.theholidayspot.com/kumbh_mela/maha_kumbh_mela.htm
- Amir Khusro - http://www.iloveindia.com/literature/urdu/poets/amir-khusro.html

Section 3.8

- Tao Te Ching - http://www.taoism.net/ttc/complete.htm
- Chuang Tzu - http://www.goodreads.com/quotes/255807-once-upon-a-time-i-dreamt-i-was-a-butterfly

Section 3.9

- Adi Shankaracharya - http://www.iloveindia.com/spirituality/gurus/adi-shankaracharya.html

Section 3.10

- Corruption Index - http://www.transparency.org/cpi2012/results
- Chinese concept of face - http://www.lifeinthefastlane.ca/china-revealed-the-concept-of-face/offbeat-news

Section 4.2

- Deng Xiaoping - http://www.economist.com/node/21533354

Section 4.4

- Manmohan Singh - http://www.preservearticles.com/201106117793/read-the-short-biography-of-dr-manmohan-singh.html

Section 4.5

- South-to-North Water Diversion Project - http://www.water-technology.net/projects/south_north/

Section 4.6

- China's solar-powered city - http://www.renewableenergyworld.com/rea/news/article/2007/05/chinas-solar-powered-city-48605

- Green Wall of China - http://en.wikipedia.org/wiki/Green_Wall_of_China

Section 4.7

- Yiwu - http://www.yiwucompany.com/yiwucompany/

Section 4.8

- Indian pharma industry - http://www.pharmaceutical-drug-manufacturers.com/pharmaceutical-industry/

Section 4.9

- Young Indian population - http://news.oneindia.in/2010/10/27/youngindian-population-an-asset-in-taking-nation-togreater.html

Section 4.10

- VOIGEN - http://domino.research.ibm.com/library/cyberdig.nsf/1e4115aea78b6e7c85256b360066f0d4/9fb1978638a52de5852572890036ddc2?OpenDocument

Section 5.1

- Change in Chinese leadership - http://www.reuters.com/article/2012/11/15/us-china-congress-idUSBRE8AD1GF20121115?feedType=RSS&feedName=topNews&utm_source=feedburner&utm_medium=feed&utm_campaign=Feed%3A+reuters%2FtopNews+%28News+%2F+US+%2F+Top+News%29&utm_content=Google+Feedfetcher

Section 5.2

- Anti-corruption party - http://world.time.com/2012/11/26/can-indias-fight-against-corruption-be-won-at-the-ballot-box/

Section 5.3

- Indian State of Emergency - http://en.wikipedia.org/wiki/State_of_Emergency_in_India

Section 5.4

- Sex disparity in China - http://www.asianews.it/news-en/Gender-disparity-increases:-121-males-born-for-every-100-women-7324.html
- China's ageing population - http://www.aljazeera.com/news/asia-pacific/2010/06/201062253642853781.html

Section 5.5
- Red corridor - http://www.aljazeera.com/programmes/aljazeeracorrespondent/2011/10/2011101974422887318.html

Section 5.6
- Military spending - http://www.globalissues.org/article/75/world-military-spending

Chapter 6
- Prognosis - http://www.businessdictionary.com/definition/prognosis.html
- The People History - http://www.thepeoplehistory.com/1988.html

Section 6.1
- G2 - http://www.globalpolicyjournal.com/articles/world-economy-trade-and-finance/g2-g-20-china-united-states-and-world-after-global-financia

Section 6.2
- Global competitiveness report - http://www3.weforum.org/docs/WEF_GlobalCompetitivenessReport_2010-11.pdf

Section 6.3
- Chinese wages - http://www.chinadaily.com.cn/cndy/2011-01/05/content_11794910.htm

Section 6.4
- Chinese leadership transition - http://www.businessinsider.com/primer-on-chinas-leadership-transition-2011-5

Section 6.5
- Khap panchayat - http://www.thehindu.com/news/national/article1710337.ece

Section 6.6
- China's 12th Five-year Plan - https://www.mckinseyquarterly.com/What_Chinas_five-year_plan_means_for_business_2832

Afterword
- Eight ways China is changing your world -
http://www.bbc.co.uk/news/world-asia-19797989

Websites *including:*
- BBC
- China Daily
- China Daily Mail
- CIA World Fact Book
- The Guardian
- The Hindu
- McKinsey Quarterly
- The New Silk Road
- New York Times
- Reuters
- South China Morning Post
- Times of India
- Wall Street Journal
- Wikipedia
- Xinhua

www.ingramcontent.com/pod-product-compliance
Lightning Source LLC
Chambersburg PA
CBHW072033190526
45165CB00017B/567